JN084347

Vitalize Your English Studies with Authentic Videos

INTEGRITY
Intermediate

mu Takeuchi   Tomoko Yabukoshi

ie Shinhara   Brent Cotsworth

KINSEIDO

Kinseido Publishing Co., Ltd.

3-21 Kanda Jimbo-cho, Chiyoda-ku,
Tokyo 101-0051, Japan

First published 2023 by Kinseido Publishing Co., Ltd.

Design   DAITECH co., ltd.

音声ファイル無料ダウンロード

https://www.kinsei-do.co.jp/download/4175

この教科書で 🎧 DL 00 の表示がある箇所の音声は、上記 URL または QR コードにて無料でダウンロードできます。自習用音声としてご活用ください。

▶ PC からのダウンロードをお勧めします。スマートフォンなどでダウンロードされる場合は、**ダウンロード前に「解凍アプリ」をインストール**してください。

▶ URL は、**検索ボックスではなくアドレスバー（URL 表示欄）**に入力してください。

▶ お使いのネットワーク環境によっては、ダウンロードできない場合があります。

◎ CD 00　左記の表示がある箇所の音声は、教室用 CD（Class Audio CD）に収録されています。

Preface

In recent years, online videos have become an integral part of daily life for many university students. Within this context, it is becoming increasingly vital that such media be used in education to excite student interest in various global topics and events, as well as to further facilitate the development of comprehension and communication skills. The three books in this series aim to provide students with next-generation texts that utilize authentic videos to integrate and enhance the four skills of English, thereby honing students' skills in both organizing and transmitting information in English.

The *INTEGRITY* series consists of three books, organized according to proficiency level as measured by TOEIC® Test: the Beginner Level is designed for the TOEIC 300–400 range, the Intermediate Level for TOEIC 400–500, and the Advanced Level for TOEIC 500–600.

As this series utilizes videos to promote deeper learning, special emphasis was placed on the selection of the videos. Across the series, several common topics were covered, including social media, AI and modern life, environmental issues, human rights issues, urban issues, gender, and life and mental health, all of which are sure to stimulate the intellectual curiosity of university students.

In addition, the series adopts a "deep-dive" approach in which each topic is carefully examined in increasing depth and from multiple perspectives. This is achieved through four phases: "Motivating Students to Learn," "Comprehension & Deeper Understanding," "Internalization & Integration," and "Output." The series is designed to first spark interest in each topic and facilitate relatively effortless content comprehension. By having students experience various topics through English, the texts provide knowledge and simultaneously facilitate critical thinking, thus vitalizing students' learning and thinking processes through both tasks and the materials themselves. At the end of each unit, students are given an opportunity to express their thoughts and opinions on the topic in English.

The writing and editing team hopes that this series will equip students with the well-balanced command of English necessary to thrive in future society.

Finally, we would like to express our sincere appreciation to the editorial team at Kinseido for their efforts in making this series possible.

Early Winter 2022

Osamu Takeuchi (Series Supervisor)
Tomoko Yabukoshi
Yukie Shinhara
Brent Cotsworth

Unit Structure

Through the following four phases, students will be able to study a single topic from multiple perspectives and deepen their knowledge and understanding of that topic.

PHASE 1 — Motivating Students to Learn

1. Getting into the Topic

This section is designed to activate background knowledge surrounding the topic covered in the unit. Students respond to fill-in-the-blank and multiple-choice questions while referring to visual information, such as graphs and photographs. The information in this section is used to assist the video viewing in the subsequent section.

2. 1st Viewing

In this section, students view a video produced by *the Guardian*—one of the world's leading media outlets—and answer multiple-choice questions. The videos are edited to be approximately 2 to 3 minutes in length.

Note: the aim is to use both visual and auditory input to understand the main ideas and key information of the video, not to pick up every detail.

PHASE 2 — Comprehension & Deeper Understanding

1. Vocabulary

Students learn key vocabulary that appears in the subsequent Reading section in a matching task. Definitions are written in simple English.

The following dictionaries were referenced for the English definitions:

Oxford Learner's Dictionary / Cambridge Dictionary / The Dictionary by Merriam-Webster / Collins Online Dictionary / Oxford Advanced Learner's Dictionary / Oxford Learner's Dictionary of Academic English

2. Reading

Students read a passage of approximately 350 words written in English. As the text includes background information and simplified explanations of the video clip viewed in Phase 1, students gain a deeper understanding of the topic. The text includes supplemental information, as well as background information not contained in the video to facilitate deeper consideration of the topic.

3. Organizer

A partially filled table, graphically representing the contents of the reading, is presented. By filling in these blanks, students review the main points of the reading while considering the structure of the English text as a whole.

PHASE 3   Internalization & Integration

2nd Viewing

The video from Phase 1 is shown again and students answer fill-in-the-blank questions that require more detailed information. Students should try to make connections with what has been learned so far. Students are sure to notice that their understanding of the video is much deeper than in the 1st Viewing.

PHASE 4   Output

Output Task

Once students are able to "own" their new knowledge, they can move on to output. Students conduct a mini-research or brainstorming session on the main theme of the unit. Subsequently, students explain what they have researched or express their own ideas either by discussing in pairs or by drafting a presentation. In the final presentation step, the checklist provided should be used as a reference for how to present while keeping the listener in mind. Only one unit (Unit 4) uses an interaction-based "consultation" session format instead of a presentation, asking students to work in pairs and give each other advice about their personal problems.

All videos have been produced by *the Guardian*.

The Guardian, which began as a weekly paper called *the Manchester Guardian* in 1821, is now one of the UK's most popular daily newspapers. It is most recognized for its investigative journalism and coverage of various social issues. In addition, its vast foreign correspondence allows it to provide stories not only domestically from the UK, but also from locations across the globe. The Guardian Media Group is like the Robin Hood of journalism, devoted to integrity and "giving a voice to the powerless and holding power to account."

Intermediate
Contents

The Future of the Meat Market

Meat-free, vegetarian burgers are making inroads in fast-food chains around the world. These burgers come with mushrooms, patties made from beans, and so on. Nowadays, plant-based fake 'meat' burgers are also available. Let's explore various kinds of meat-free products and think about which one is popular among consumers.

PHASE 1

1 | Getting into the Topic

Read part of the website of an Australia-based company called v2food. Fill in the blanks with the appropriate phrases from below.

OUR MISSION

In 2050, the world population is predicted to hit [1] _____.

We need to create a version 2 of meat if we're going to feed our growing population in a way that

[2] _____.

v2 is the delicious, healthy option for anyone who loves the taste of meat but doesn't want to get it

[3] _____. We've designed our v2 products to look, cook, and taste just like meat so that

[4] _____ is all gain, no pain.

---

takes care of our planet	going plant-based	10 billion people	from animals

2 🎥 1st Viewing

online/video

Watch the video and choose the best answers to the following questions.

1. What is being held in the video?
   a. A cooking contest
   b. A tasting session
   c. A product planning meeting

2. How many kinds of burgers are introduced in the video?
   a. Three
   b. Four
   c. Five

PHASE 2

1 📋 Vocabulary

Match the words with their definitions.

1. **veggie** [   ]   a. the part of a plant that is eaten as a vegetable, dark red in color
2. **patty** [   ]
3. **chickpea** [   ]   b. to emit or let out liquid
4. **scientifically-engineered** [   ]   c. containing no meat or fish
5. **bleed** [   ]   d. a round bean that can be cooked and eaten
6. **beetroot** [   ]   e. not having a strong or interesting taste or flavor
7. **bland** [   ]   f. a small flat cake of finely chopped food
                         g. created using systematic and organized methods

2 📖 Reading

🎧 DL 02   CD 02

Read the following passage.

What do Meat-Free Burgers Taste like?

Vegetarian options are becoming available in major fast-food chains around the world. Particularly, plant-based fake 'meat' burgers have attracted people's attention. Alyx Gorman, a lifestyle editor of *the Guardian*, held a tasting session of four types of meat-free, vegetarian burgers. Four *Guardian* staffers attended the session.

5   The tasters started with a Mary's mushroom veggie burger, which comes with a big old slice of portobello mushroom. This burger seemed to be more or less satisfying. One taster said, "That's really good." The group then tried a Ribs & Burgers' traditional veggie patty burger. The patty is made from chickpeas. This burger also seemed to be mostly acceptable. While one taster commented on the good taste of the chickpeas, another pointed out that

10   beans all have a very similar taste and said, "unless you kind of get a burger that's very spicy, it's kind of hard to get beyond those—that taste."

The group then tasted two kinds of scientifically-engineered fake 'meat' burgers. One burger was from Ribs & Burgers, featuring a patty made by Beyond Meat, a US-based company that offers plant-based 'meat' products. The patty bleeds like meat, using fake beetroot blood.

15   While one taster seemed to be impressed with the way it looks, another did not, describing it as "a little bit disturbing." Other comments included "That's not bad," and "I don't mind that." The last burger was from Hungry Jack's. This burger comes with a patty made by v2food, an Australia's plant-based 'meat' company. The v2food plant-based 'meat' patty is co-created with CSIRO, an Australian national science agency. It looked like this burger attracted kind of

20   unfavorable comments from the tasters. One taster described it as "bland."

Companies are currently working hard on improving the tastes of plant-based 'meat' products, and fast-food chains are trying to promote plant-based fake 'meat' burgers across the globe. In Japan, Mos Burger has released the Mos Plant-Based 'Green Burger.' This burger comes with a patty made from a mix of soybeans, *konnyaku* and cabbage. Other

25   major hamburger chains like Freshness Burger and Lotteria have also introduced soybean-based burgers. Do these fake 'meat' burgers taste just as good as regular meat burgers? It will be interesting to see who will win the meat-free burger market in the end.

375 words

Notes

ℓ 5   **Mary's:** a group that has opened bar/restaurants and takeaway stores in Australia

ℓ 6   **portobello:** a large rich-flavored brown mushroom used in cooking

ℓ 7   **Ribs & Burgers:** an Australian fast-food restaurant chain

ℓ 17 **Hungry Jack's:** an Australian fast-food chain

ℓ 19 **CSIRO:** the abbreviation for 'Commonwealth Scientific and Industrial Research Organisation'

ℓ 23 **Green Burger:** This burger is available, as of September 2022.

Intermediate

3 📄 Organizer

Fill in each blank and complete the organizer based on the information from the reading.

Guardian's Taste Test Hosted by Ms. [1] _____

Kind	Shop	Feature	Reaction / Comments
Mushroom Burger 	*Mary's*	A big old slice of [2] _____ mushroom	[3] _____ That's really good.
Veggie Patty Burger	[4] _____	Patty made from [5] _____	Mostly acceptable
[6] _____ -Based Fake 'Meat' Burger	*Ribs & Burgers*	Patty made by Beyond Meat, using fake beetroot blood	A little bit [7] _____
	Hungry Jack's	Patty co-created by v2food & [8] _____	Kind of unfavorable Bland

PHASE 3

▶️ 2nd Viewing

(online / video)

Watch the video again and complete the answers to the following questions.

1. What is Ms. Smythe's comment on the mushroom burger?

She says, "it's a perfectly-acceptable _____ , you know."

2. What does Ms. Spring say about the Ribs & Burgers' traditional veggie patty burger?

She says that it is just like a really good chickpea thing, but it is _____

_____ a burger.

3. What does the Ribs & Burgers' fake meat burger taste like to Mr. Earley?

It actually tastes like _____ to him.

PHASE 4

💬✎ Output Task (Writing / Speaking)

Plant-based meat products are making inroads in Japan. Create a report and make a presentation about one plant-based meat product.

Step 1 ▶ Answer the following questions.

a. What plant-based meat product are you going to report on?

Type: _____

e.g., a plant-based meat sandwich

b. What is the product name?

Name: _____

*e.g., "Whole Grain Sandwich Soy Meat" *as of September 2022*

c. Where is it available? Or, which company has produced it?

Shop/Restaurant/Manufacturer: _____

e.g., Doutor, a Japanese coffee shop chain

d. What features does the product have?

Features: _____

e.g., a plant-based meat made from soybeans, coming with kinpira burdock and yuzu pepper soy milk sauce

Step 2 Write a report (about 40 words) about the product. Use the information you answered in Step 1.

I am going to report on _____

_____

_____

_____

> e.g., I am going to report on a plant-based meat sandwich. Doutor, a Japanese coffee shop chain, has released "Whole Grain Sandwich Soy Meat." It features a plant-based meat made from soybeans. It comes with kinpira burdock and yuzu pepper soy milk sauce.

Step 3 Practice the report that you made in Step 2. Then, present the report to the class.

Checklist for the Presentation

Use this checklist to evaluate one of your classmate's presentations.

		Good				Bad
1.	The speaker speaks in correct sentence forms.	☐ 5	☐ 4	☐ 3	☐ 2	☐ 1
2.	The speaker provides the basic information (i.e., type, name, shop, etc.) of the product clearly.	☐ 5	☐ 4	☐ 3	☐ 2	☐ 1
3.	The speaker describes the features of the product.	☐ 5	☐ 4	☐ 3	☐ 2	☐ 1
4.	The speaker makes eye contact with the audience.	☐ 5	☐ 4	☐ 3	☐ 2	☐ 1

UNIT 2

The Road to a Carbon-Free World

Nowadays, although electric vehicles are convenient, cost and lack of charging places are a barrier to those who try to purchase them. Let's look at how countries are working to shift to electric vehicles.

PHASE 1

1 Getting into the Topic

Read the ad of an electric car. Fill in the blanks with the appropriate words from below. Change the lowercase letters into the capitals where needed.

Go Green with Clean Energy **It's time to shift to EV!**

$60,000

Get a [1] _____ with the government incentive program!

Free of Cost Installation of Fast [2] _____

[3] _____ : 350km in a single charge

[4] _____ **Costs**: Less than $3.00 per 100km

charger	discount	running	range

2 📹 1st Viewing

Watch the video and choose the best answers to the following questions.

1. How much of the total carbon emissions is the Australian Transport Sector made up of?

   a. 9%

   b. 19%

   c. 29%

2. Which country has succeeded in implementing electric vehicles?

   a. Australia

   b. Netherlands

   c. Norway

PHASE 2

1 📋 Vocabulary

Match the words with their definitions.

1. **emissions**	[ ]	**a.**	to prevent someone from doing something or make them not want to do it
2. **accelerate**	[ ]	**b.**	a part of an area of activity, especially of a country's economy or business
3. **sector**	[ ]	**c.**	something (e.g., a payment) that encourages a person to do something
4. **vague**	[ ]	**d.**	an amount of gas, heat, light, etc. that is sent out into the air
5. **deter**	[ ]	**e.**	to form part of something, especially a larger group
6. **incentive**	[ ]	**f.**	to start to move or drive faster
7. **comprise**	[ ]	**g.**	not clear or uncertain

2 📖 Reading

 DL 03   ⦿ CD 03

Read the following passage.

Spreading Electric Vehicles: Challenges to Overcome

    Australia is one of the world's biggest carbon emitters per capita and is under pressure from the international community to start cutting emissions. In fact, more and more developed
³ nations are on an accelerating course toward net zero emissions by 2050. At a recent global

climate summit, Scott Morrison, the Australian Prime Minister at the time, also announced a
5   plan to achieve net zero emissions by 2050.

One way to achieve this is to target the transport sector. According to *the Guardian*,
the Australian transport sector is responsible for 19% of all the nation's carbon emissions.
Dr. Anna Mortimore, a university lecturer who is an expert on transportation, believes that
the only way to reduce transport emissions down to zero is to use electric vehicles. However,
10   the market for electric vehicles in Australia is tiny, with only 5,875 vehicles purchased out
of a total of over a million vehicles in 2019. In other words, Australians still do not want to
buy electric vehicles though they are quieter, more efficient, more reliable, and better for the
environment. Why could that be?

The first reason for this is the price. For example, the electric version of a Hyundai Kona,
15   a popular vehicle in Australia, is around $25,000 more expensive than the petrol version.
Another reason is that many Australians suffer from something called "range anxiety." That
is something like vague concerns that the car's battery will run out before they reach their
destination. Such psychological barriers deter consumers from electric vehicles. It should also
be noted that electric vehicle charging points are still rare compared to petrol stations.

20   If the government takes action now, many of these problems could be fixed. However,
more can be done to promote electric vehicles, as Dr. Mortimore suggests. One example
is giving incentives such as allowing electric vehicles to use the bus lane. This was highly
successful in Norway, and the country has been a global leader in switching to electric
vehicles. Another example is Germany. In 2020, they doubled incentives for electric vehicles,
25   and this resulted in a dramatic increase in the number of EVs on the road.

What can we learn from cases of other countries? It is time for every country to play a
role in achieving a carbon-free society.

377 words

Notes

ℓ1   **per capita:** for each person; in relation to people taken individually

ℓ3   **net zero emissions:** achieving an overall balance between greenhouse gas emissions produced and greenhouse gas emissions taken out of the atmosphere

ℓ3   **global climate summit:** The 26th United Nations Climate Change Conference (COP26) held from 31 October to 13 November 2021 in Glasgow, Scotland

ℓ4   **Scott Morrison:** a former Prime Minister of Australia (2018-2022)

ℓ16   **range anxiety:** the driver's fear that a vehicle has insufficient energy storage (fuel and/or electric) to cover the road distance needed to reach its intended destination

3 📄 Organizer

Fill in each blank and complete the organizer based on the information from the reading.

EVs: Problems and Suggestions

Why EVs?

- ⊙ At a recent global climate ¹_____, the Australian Prime Minister at the time annouced 'net zero-emissions' by 2050.
- ⊙ To achieve the goal, the target is the transport sector.
- ⊙ EVs are quieter, more ²_____, more reliable, and better for the environment.

The Problems

Why the ³_____ for EVs in Australia is tiny

- ⊙ Price
  └ the electric version of a Hyundai Kona = $⁴_____ more expensive than the petrol version
- ⊙ Suffering from range anxiety
- ⊙ Finding the ⁵_____ points

Experts' Suggestions

The government should...

- ⊙ take ⁶_____ now to fix the above problems.
- ⊙ give incentives:
  e.g., allowing electric vehicles to use the ⁷_____ lane
      giving financial incentives for the purchase of EVs

PHASE 3

■◀ 2nd Viewing

Watch the video again and complete the answers to the following questions.

1. In Australia, how many electric vehicles were sold last year?

Only _____ electric vehicles were sold.

2. According to Dr. Anna Mortimore, what is range anxiety?

It is when people think about how far they drive, and look at the _____ of the

_____ that they have in their vehicle.

3. How did Norway succeed in promoting the EVs?

In Norway, they allow electric vehicle owners to drive in the bus lane, which is also known as a

non-financial _____ .

PHASE 4

💬✎ Output Task (Writing / Speaking)

We all know that electric vehicles are convenient and may be the key to slowing climate change. Do some research about potential barriers to purchasing EVs and suggest a solution which encourages the spread of the vehicles. Then, make a presentation in class.

Step I ▶ Answer the following questions.

a. What is the disadvantage/difficulty of having an electric vehicle in your country?

Disadvantage: _____

e.g., the price

b. What is the solution for that problem?

Solution: _____

e.g., to make it cheap

Step 2 Write down the findings about electric vehicles. Then, suggest a solution which encourages the spread of the EVs.

I found that a problem with electric vehicles is _____

_____ .

However, by _____ ,

the use of electric vehicles might spread.

Step 3 Practice the report that you made in Step 2. Then, present the report to the class.

Checklist for the Presentation

Use this checklist to evaluate one of your classmate's presentations.

		Good				Bad
1.	The speaker speaks in correct sentence forms.	5	4	3	2	1
2.	The speaker explains the problem clearly.	5	4	3	2	1
3.	The speaker provides a solution to the problem.	5	4	3	2	1
4.	The speaker makes eye contact with the audience.	5	4	3	2	1

UNIT 3

The Meaning of a Healthy Lifestyle

People have become more and more health-conscious. They are promoting a healthy lifestyle through social media, such as Instagram and Twitter, with hashtags of "eatclean" and "cleaneating." What does it mean to eat clean? Let's explore it and consider what a healthy lifestyle is.

PHASE 1

1 | Getting into the Topic

Look at the photos shared on social media with a hashtag of "eat clean" (#eatclean). Fill in the blanks in the captions with the appropriate words from below.

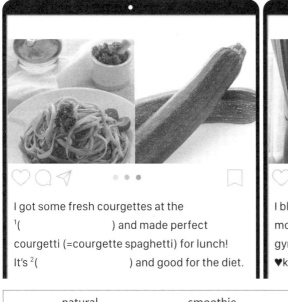

I got some fresh courgettes at the [1](   ) and made perfect courgetti (=courgette spaghetti) for lunch! It's [2](   ) and good for the diet.

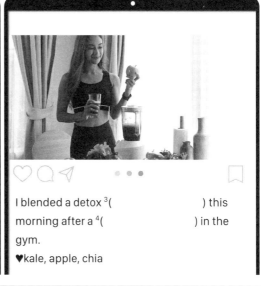

I blended a detox [3](   ) this morning after a [4](   ) in the gym.
♥kale, apple, chia

natural	smoothie	market	workout

2 | ■◀ 1st Viewing

online video

Watch the video and choose the best answers to the following questions.

1. What did the female speaker in the video find in the gym changing room?
   a. A woman crying a lot
   b. A woman drinking a smoothie
   c. A woman taking a selfie (i.e., a photo of herself)

2. What kinds of Instagram photos have been introduced in the video?
   a. Food, drinks, and young women
   b. The latest fast fashion brands
   c. Healthy restaurants

PHASE 2

1 | 📋 Vocabulary

Match the words with their definitions.

1. **purity** [ ]
2. **toxic** [ ]
3. **chronic** [ ]
4. **nutrition** [ ]
5. **demonization** [ ]
6. **pursuit** [ ]
7. **obsession** [ ]

a. food that you need to be healthy and grow
b. describing any condition that lasts for a long time; difficult to cure or treat
c. the state in which your mind is full of one particular thing
d. an act of looking for or achieving something
e. the state or quality of not being mixed with anything else
f. containing poison that may cause illness or death
g. the act of describing something as evil or dangerous

2 | 📖 Reading

DL 04   CD 04

Read the following passage.

Is #cleaneating Actually Making Us Clean?

Have you ever heard of "clean eating?" This expression emerged in the mid-2000s, when fitness models and Instagram influencers began promoting vegan, sugar-free, unprocessed
3   natural foods. As they posted photographs of fruit bowls and raw kale smoothies on their

Instagram feeds, they encouraged purity in a world full of "toxic" food. The message behind
⁵ these photos could be, "if you eat a 'clean' diet, you can achieve a body like mine."

In the beginning, the clean eating movement focused mainly on people with chronic
health problems. They changed their eating habits to see if their conditions would improve.
In the absence of nutrition guidance from experts, it was a natural step for people to start
experimenting with cutting out this food or that completely. One example of this is the
¹⁰ demonization of gluten. Between 2009 and 2015, the number of Americans who actively
avoided gluten is said to have tripled, despite the fact that most of them were not suffering
from disease related to gluten intake.

Nowadays, social media has spread the clean eating movement even further. The most
popular lifestyle Instagrammers released recipe books, teaching the public how to eat clean.
¹⁵ When Ella Woodward, a UK health and lifestyle blogger with a million Instagram followers,
released a recipe book in 2015, she sold 32,000 copies in the first week alone.

Actually, many experts believe that the pursuit of "purity of eating" is addictive and could
even be dangerous for people's health. Cutting out entire food groups means the body cannot
obtain all the nutrition it needs. One shocking example is that one Instagrammer's hair fell
²⁰ out from eating a restricted "clean" diet. Scientists have called the obsession with clean eating
"orthorexia." Although orthorexia affects both men and women, the fact that the clean eating
movement is promoted so much on Instagram by perfect-looking models means that women
and teenagers are the ones most likely to be influenced.

Rather than aiming to eat "clean," experts in nutrition all agree that we should aim for
²⁵ a balanced diet. They say that food should
never be divided into "clean" and "dirty"
categories.

350 words

Notes

ℓ 2 **vegan:** not eating, using, or including any food or products from animals

ℓ 10 **gluten:** a protein that is contained in grains such as wheat

ℓ 21 **orthorexia:** an unhealthy focus on eating only healthy foods

3 📄 Organizer

Fill in each blank and complete the organizer based on the information from the reading.

Clean Eating Movement

Background

- The expression of "clean eating" emerged in the mid-2000s.
- People started...
  ▶promoting ¹_____, sugar-free, unprocessed natural foods on Instagram, etc.
  ▶encouraging ²_____ in a world full of "toxic" food.

In the beginning

- The movement focused mainly on people with chronic health problems.
- People started cutting out this food or that completely.
  e.g., the demonization of ³_____

Nowadays

- The movement has spread through ⁴_____ media.
  e.g., the release of recipe books by the most popular lifestyle Instagrammers

Experts' Opinions

- The pursuit of "purity of eating" can become addictive and dangerous for people's health. e.g., hair falling out
- There will be the risk of "orthorexia."
  └Influencing, in particular,
  ⁵_____ and teenagers

Health Concerns

- People should aim for a balanced diet.
- People should not divide food into "clean" and "⁶_____" categories.

Suggestions

PHASE 3

📹 2nd Viewing

Watch the video again and complete the answers to the following questions.

1. What does the female speaker in the video say about chia seed smoothie?

She says, "If you didn't take a photo of your chia seed smoothie, did you even _____

_____ _____ ?"

2. What do hashtags of "eat clean" (#eatclean) and "nourish yourself" (#nourishyourself) mean?

These hashtags mean big business for _____ , apps, and _____

clothes brands.

3. What does the speaker suggest about eating healthily?

It is good, but taking it too far can actually be _____ .

PHASE 4

💬✎ Output Task (Writing / Speaking)

Let's think about what healthy eating means to you and make yourself a meal plan.
Then, share your answers with a partner and make a presentation in class.

Step 1 Give a definition of healthy eating and make yourself a meal plan for this
Sunday. Answer the following two questions.

a. What does healthy eating mean to you?

Definition: _____

e.g., Cutting out fatty foods

b. What would you like to eat this Sunday? Based on your definition above, make a meal plan for this
Sunday. List at least three dishes for each meal.

Sunday Meal Plan		
Breakfast	**Lunch**	**Dinner**
•	•	•
•	•	•
•	•	•
e.g., Low-fat yogurt, etc.	*e.g., Seafood rice bowl, etc.*	*e.g., Boiled tofu, etc.*

Step 2 ▶ Share your answers with your partner. Ask the two questions from the previous page and write down your partner's answers.

My partner defines healthy eating as _____

_____ . This Sunday, he/she will eat _____

_____ for breakfast,

_____ for lunch, and

_____ for dinner.

Step 3 ▶ Practice the report that you made in Step 2. Then, present the report to the class.

Checklist for the Presentation

Use this checklist to evaluate one of your classmate's presentations.

		Good				Bad
1.	The speaker speaks in correct sentence forms.	5	4	3	2	1
2.	The speaker explains his/her partner's definition clearly.	5	4	3	2	1
3.	The speaker describes his/her partner's meal plan in some detail.	5	4	3	2	1
4.	The speaker makes eye contact with the audience.	5	4	3	2	1

UNIT 4

Keys to a Successful Job Interview

Some people are not good at talking in front of people. They may become nervous when they make presentations, have job interviews, or take interview exams, etc. When you feel a lot of stress and get stuck, what would you do? If you cannot find solutions on your own, it is probably a good idea to talk to someone else.

PHASE 1

1 Getting into the Topic

The following are common questions at a job interview and model answers to them. Fill in the blanks with the appropriate words from below to complete the model answers.

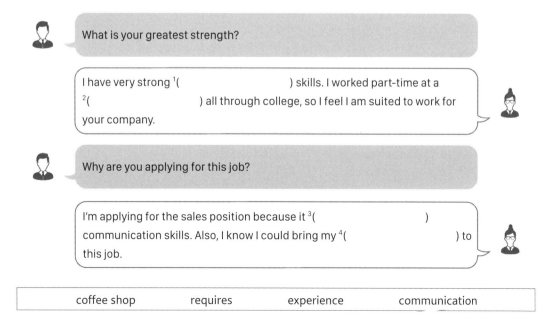

What is your greatest strength?

I have very strong [1]( ) skills. I worked part-time at a [2]( ) all through college, so I feel I am suited to work for your company.

Why are you applying for this job?

I'm applying for the sales position because it [3]( ) communication skills. Also, I know I could bring my [4]( ) to this job.

coffee shop	requires	experience	communication

2 📹 1st Viewing

online video

Watch the video and choose the best answers to the following questions.

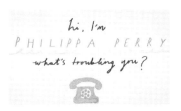

1. What is the caller mainly talking about?

   a. Her school life

   b. Her future plans

   c. Her concerns

2. What is this woman doing?

   a. Offering advice

   b. Getting feedback

   c. Calling her friend

PHASE 2

1 📋 Vocabulary

Match the words with their definitions.

1. **incredibly**	[ ]	**a.** a person who treats mental illness
2. **nerves**	[ ]	**b.** to accept or recognize that something is true
3. **qualified**	[ ]	**c.** feelings of worry, anxiety, or pressure
4. **psychotherapist**	[ ]	**d.** to a much greater degree; extremely
5. **agony aunt**	[ ]	**e.** to behave so as to make other people believe something that is not true
6. **pretend**	[ ]	**f.** having particular skills to do something
7. **acknowledge**	[ ]	**g.** a person, especially a woman, who offers people advice

2 📖 Reading

 DL 05   CD 05

Read the following passage.

Shall We Dance? — Ultimate Job Interview Tip for You

A job interview can be an incredibly stressful experience. According to a survey conducted at Everest College in the US, 9 out of 10 adults find something about an interview
3   stressful. Around 17% of respondents said nerves were their biggest fear, while 15% said

that they worried about being too qualified for the job. Being underqualified for the role
was another common fear, while not being able to answer the interviewer's questions was
also mentioned as something that caused interview anxiety. It seems that although interview
anxiety is common, sometimes it can be so bad that it has an impact on a person's ability to
get a job.

One such woman called *the Guardian*'s psychotherapist and agony aunt Philippa Perry
for advice about the extreme anxiety she feels whenever she has to attend job interviews.
The caller explained that she feels like she is pretending to be someone else in interviews. As
a student, she had a number of part-time jobs but did not take her previous jobs seriously.
Because of that, she feels like she does not know how to tell potential employers about her
positive personal qualities in interviews.

Philippa's advice is to first acknowledge that all people are pretending in interviews.
In her words, interviews are a "dance" involving the interviewer and the interviewee, so the
interviewee must put on their public face, also known as their "game face" and show only the
positive sides of their personality. In fact, research has shown that putting on a determined
expression, or "game face" before an important event, such as an interview or sports event,
may have a positive influence on both mood and performance. In life, it is natural to have a
private face and an edited version of yourself for public. We accept that quite naturally in our
everyday lives, but Phillipa suggests that the interviewee's brain is often "short-circuiting" a
bit when it comes to interviews. She goes on to say the caller should try to shift her focus away
from the former version of herself and move toward a new idea of what she can achieve now.
The most important thing, as Phillipa puts it, is to enjoy the "game" during interviews.

367 words

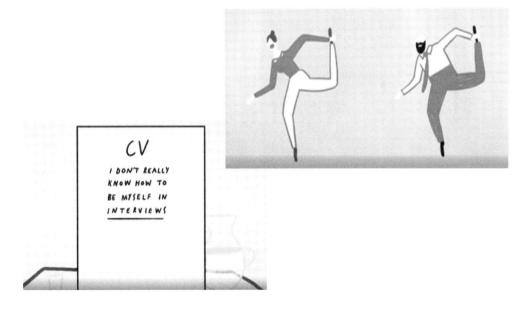

3 📄 Organizer

Fill in each blank and complete the organizer based on the information from the reading.

Problems with and Advice for a Job Interview

Background
- ❯ A job interview can be an incredibly ¹_____ experience.
- ❯ Interview ²_____ has an impact on a person's ability to get a job.

Caller

A woman

Receiver

Philippa Perry
└*The Guardian*'s psychotherapist and agony aunt

↔

The Caller's Problems
- ❯ She feels extreme ²_____ in job interviews.
- ▷ She feels like she is pretending to be someone else.
- ▷ She did not take her previous part-time jobs seriously and does not know how to tell her ³_____ personal qualities.

The Receiver's Advice
- ❯ Interviews are a "⁴_____" involving the interviewer and the interviewee.

Interviewees must...
- ▷ put on their public face (i.e., "game face").
- ▷ show only the positive sides of their personality.

The caller should...
- ▷ shift her focus away from the ⁵_____ version of herself and move toward a new idea of what she can achieve now.
- ▷ most importantly, enjoy the "⁶_____" during interviews.

PHASE 3

📹◀ 2nd Viewing

(online / video)

Watch the video again and complete the answers to the following questions.

1. In the opening of the video, what does Philippa say to the caller to ask about her problems?

   She asks, "What's _____ you?"

2. According to the caller, what issues has she always had at her previous jobs?

   She has always had issues with being _____ or not _____

   _____ for work.

3. What does Phillipa say about the old idea of oneself as unreliable?

   She says that it is not some ultimate _____ .

PHASE 4

💬✍ Output Task (Writing / Speaking)

Write about your problem and discuss it with a partner.

Step 1 ▶ Write about a problem that you are currently facing. This can be a problem at school, at home, at work, or anywhere else.

_____

_____

e.g., I have so many things to do at school, and I am stuck.

Step 2 Based on the incomplete dialogue below, take turns being Student A and Student B and talk about your problem with your partner. After the conversation, fill in the blanks.

1. Student A asks Student B's problem.
2. Student B talks about his/her problem and asks for advice.
3. Student A gives some advice.

A: *What's troubling you?*

B: _____

_____

Is there any advice you could offer me?

A: _____

_____

Step 3 Exchange your roles and complete the dialogue below.

1. Student B asks Student A's problem.
2. Student A talks about his/her problem and asks for advice.
3. Student B gives some advice.

B: *What's troubling you?*

A: _____

_____

Is there any advice you could offer me?

B: _____

_____

UNIT 5

The Healing Power of Animals

We see animals everywhere in our daily lives, and animals help people in various ways. Animal therapy, also called pet therapy or animal-assisted therapy, is one method to help people recover from some physical or mental health conditions.

PHASE 1

1 | Getting into the Topic

Read the explanation of animal-assisted therapy. Fill in the blanks with the appropriate words from below.

Animal-assisted therapy (AAT) is a type of therapy that involves animals as a form of
[1]( ). Therapy dogs face their patients' mental and physical situations together with the patients and assist them in [2]( ) the patients' mental and physical functions.

AAT has been used for...
e.g.,
- Children having dental procedures
- People with diseases such as
  [3]( ) and stroke
- Nurses and doctors with high [4]( ) levels

stress	improving	treatment	cancer

Intermediate

2  1st Viewing

Watch the video and choose the best answers to the following questions.

1. What are these women most likely doing?
   a. Walking dogs
   b. Training dogs
   c. Feeding dogs

2. According to this woman, where do dogs work for people?
   a. Hotels
   b. Restaurants
   c. Hospitals

PHASE 2

1 Vocabulary

Match the words with their definitions.

1. **care facility**   [   ]   a. the fact that you are with someone
2. **immediately**   [   ]   b. without taking something or somebody into account
3. **temperament**   [   ]   c. now or without being late
4. **equipment**   [   ]   d. a place built to provide what people need for their health
5. **company**   [   ]   e. to meet somebody in an unexpected way
6. **regardless of**   [   ]   f. tools or machinery that you need for a particular purpose
7. **encounter**   [   ]   g. an animal's nature as shown in the way they behave in response to situations

2 Reading DL 06   CD 06

Read the following passage.

Animal-Assisted Therapy in New York

It has been known for a long time that spending time with animals makes humans happy. There is also increasing evidence that having an animal around can have beneficial health
3   effects, such as lowering blood pressure or the risk of heart disease. That is why more and

more hospitals and care facilities are using therapy dogs. Many volunteers describe the fact
that whenever they introduce a therapy dog to patients, staff and children immediately smile.
However, dogs that go on to become therapy animals must have the correct temperament.
Renee Payne, who teaches dog training classes at the Good Dog Foundation based in New
York, admits that the hardest thing for dogs is to approach a wheelchair. A hospital room with
cold, metal wheelchairs or noisy medical equipment can be scary for dogs, so they need to be
trained not to react negatively.

In the early 2000s, therapy animals were not permitted to enter hospitals in New York.
Thanks to efforts by organizations such as the Good Dog Foundation, the law has been
changed and today, some hospitals in New York even allow patients to bring their own pets
from home. Michele Siegel, who works at New York Therapy Animals, another organization,
says that any kind of dog is welcome to join her class for therapy dogs. The most important
thing, she states, is that the dog enjoys the company of humans. The dogs she trains make
people's faces light up. The fact that she gets that reaction makes her job worthwhile.

Because of the positive effect therapy dogs can have on people's mental health, they
are increasingly used in various settings other than hospitals. New York Therapy Animals
is involved in a unique program that sends dogs to schools to act as "reading assistants" for
children who have trouble learning to read. The children like the idea of "reading to a dog"
and become highly motivated in their studies. Experts hope that animal-assisted therapy will
expand far beyond hospital rooms, as dogs offer unconditional love to people regardless of
their backgrounds. In the not-so-distant future, you
may encounter therapy dogs in schools, hospitals,
restaurants, or other facilities!

358 words

Notes

ℓ 7   **The Good Dog Foundation:** an organization providing therapy dog services

ℓ 14 **New York Therapy Animals:** an organization offering a therapy dog education and training program

Intermediate

3  Organizer

Fill in each blank and complete the organizer based on the information from the reading.

Therapy Animals/Dogs in N.Y.

Concepts of Using Therapy Animals/Dogs

- Spending time with animals makes humans happy.
- Having an animal around can have beneficial
  1 _____ effects.

Becoming Therapy Animals/Dogs

There are dog training classes in N.Y.

e.g.,

- Classes taught by 2 _____ at the Good Dog Foundation
- Classes taught by Michele Siegel at New York Therapy Animals

Therapy Animals/Dogs in Various Settings

Hospitals	**Other than Hospitals**
- Patients are even allowed to bring their own 3 _____ to some hospitals.	- Dogs are sent to schools to act as "4 _____" for children.

The Future of Therapy Animals/Dogs

Therapy dogs may be used in schools, hospitals, 5 _____, or other facilities.

PHASE 3

▄◀ 2nd Viewing

Watch the video again and complete the answers to the following questions.

1. According to Renee Payne, what is "Therapy 2"?

It is a real _____ _____ class.

2. What does Renee Payne indicate about a wheelchair?

Learning to _____ a wheelchair is the _____ thing for dogs.

3. According to Michele Siegel, what type of dog is welcome to join her class?

Any dog that enjoys the company of _____ is welcome to join her class.

PHASE 4

💬✓ Output Task (Writing / Speaking)

As in New York, animal therapy has been promoted in Japan. Do some research about animal therapy in Japan and write down two facts that you have learned about it. Then, share your findings with a partner and make a presentation in class.

Step I Do some research about animal therapy in Japan and write down two facts that you have learned about it on the next page.

> e.g., • Are there any organizations which provide animal therapy in Japan?
> • Which facilities or institutes are using therapy animals/dogs in Japan?
> • How can we become an animal therapist in Japan?

FINDINGS

- _____

_____

- _____

_____

---

e.g., • There are several organizations, such as..., which provide animal therapy in Japan.

• Several facilities or institutes, such as..., are using therapy animals/dogs in Japan.

• It looks like it is not necessary to have a license to become an animal therapist in Japan, but it is recommended to....

Step 2 Share your findings with your partner. Ask questions like *"What did you find out about animal therapy in Japan?"* and write down your partner's answers.

My partner found that _____

_____ .

He/She also found that _____

_____ .

Step 3 Practice the report that you made in Step 2. Then, present the report to the class.

Checklist for the Presentation

Use this checklist to evaluate one of your classmate's presentations.

		Good				Bad
1.	The speaker speaks in correct sentence forms.	5	4	3	2	1
2.	The speaker explains his/her partner's findings clearly.	5	4	3	2	1
3.	The speaker describes the findings in some detail.	5	4	3	2	1
4.	The speaker makes eye contact with the audience.	5	4	3	2	1

Measures to Help Job Seekers

Several support measures have been provided by the government or organizations for people to meet basic human needs (i.e., food, housing, health, and education). In Australia, a range of income support payments, such as Newstart Allowance,* help people with living costs.

*It was replaced by and renamed JobSeeker Payment on March 20, 2020.

PHASE 1

 **1** Getting into the Topic

Read the brief explanation of "JobSeeker Payment." Fill in the blanks with the appropriate words from below.

◎ *What is "JobSeeker Payment"?*

> It is a form of financial help for ¹( ) workers in Australia. It replaced Newstart Allowance [mentioned in the video] when it was stopped in March 2020.

◎ *Who will get the service?*

> You need to meet several rules.
> e.g.,
> • You're ²( ) 22 and Age Pension age.
> • You're looking for work. It's also for when you're sick or ³( ) and can't do your usual work or ⁴( ) for a short time.

unemployed	between	study	injured

2 | ◼◀ 1st Viewing

Watch the video and choose the best answers to the following questions.

1. Who most likely are these people?

    a. Politicians

    b. News reporters

    c. Professors

2. What seems to be a problem with Newstart Allowance?

    a. The period of the payment

    b. The amount of the payment

    c. The method of the payment

PHASE 2

1 | 📋 Vocabulary

Match the words with their definitions.

1. allowance	[ ]	**a.** officially agreed or accepted
2. approved	[ ]	**b.** changes and improvements that are made to a system, an organization, etc.
3. recipient	[ ]	
4. edible	[ ]	**c.** to fix something, such as pay and prices, at a particular level and not allow any increases; a decision to do so
5. freeze	[ ]	**d.** money that is given to someone in order to help them pay for necessary things
6. welfare	[ ]	**e.** help or support given, often by the government, to people who need it
7. reform	[ ]	**f.** safe for eating and not harmful
		g. a person who gets or is provided something

2 | 📖 Reading

 DL 07    CD 07

Read the following passage.

Newstart Allowance: A Way to Help People in Need?

    Newstart Allowance was introduced in Australia in 1991. The allowance was an income support payment for people aged 22 or older, but under Age Pension age. The payment
3 financially helped people who were unemployed or treated as unemployed, while they looked

for work, participated in approved activities to increase their chances of getting a job, and so

5 on.

In 2019, there appeared to be a growing movement to raise Newstart Allowance. One issue was that the amount of the payment was not likely to meet the recipients' living costs. At that moment, a single person on Newstart received $277.85 a week. A *Guardian* reporter, Luke Henriques-Gomes, reported that the amount of Newstart Allowance was so low that many

10 recipients might not have money to get to a job interview. The reporter also mentioned that they were not likely to have enough money for food. One recipient said that she had actually kind of picked through the food for her chickens to see if there was anything edible for her that night. Another issue was that Newstart Allowance had not had a real increase since 1994. John Howard had essentially frozen Newstart in 1997. He even said in an interview afterward

15 that the freeze had gone on too long.

It looked like several politicians called for the increase of Newstart Allowance. For example, Rachel Siewert claimed that the allowance had not been increased for many years. Barnaby Joyce stressed that the amount of the payment was not enough. Pauline Hanson was in favor of lifting the rate of the allowance. However, the Prime Minister at that time,

20 Scott Morrison, and some ministers were seemingly against raising the payment. Rather than increasing the payment, they probably focused on helping unemployed people get jobs, saying "the best form of welfare is a job."

In March 2020, Newstart Allowance was replaced by and renamed JobSeeker Payment, as part of the payment reform. The payment has

25 been increased, but there seem to be many people who cannot afford their living costs. It is hoped that the government will continue the reform and provide better support to help people in need.

355 words

Notes

ℓ 2 **Age Pension:** the main income support payment for people who have reached Age Pension age that is 66 years and 6 months or older, as of September 2022

ℓ 14 **John Howard:** a former Prime Minister of Australia (1996-2007)

ℓ 17 **Rachel Siewert:** a former senator for Western Australia, a state of Australia (2005-2021)

ℓ 18 **Barnaby Joyce:** a former leader of the Nationals (i.e., an Australian political party, formally known as the National Party of Australia)

ℓ 18 **Pauline Hanson:** a senator for Queensland, a state of Australia, as of September 2022

ℓ 20 **Scott Morrison:** a former Prime Minister of Australia (2018-2022)

3 | Organizer

Fill in each blank and complete the organizer based on the information from the reading.

Newstart Allowance

Type	An [1] _____ support payment for people unemployed or treated as unemployed
Recipient Age	[2] _____ years or older but under Age Pension age
Amount	$ [3] _____ / week in 2019

Issues	• Not likely to meet the recipients' living costs
	    e.g., Unable to get to a job interview
	        Not to have enough money for [4] _____
	
	• No real increase of the payment since 1994 and being frozen too long

Politicians' Opinions	• Several politicians: Calling for the increase • [5] _____ at that time and some ministers: Against the increase
Reform	Replacing and renaming Newstart Allowance → [6] _____ Payment in March 2020

PHASE 3

📹 2nd Viewing

 online video

Watch the video again and complete the answers to the following questions.

1. What does Pauline Hanson mean, when she says, "Yes, I do?"

She thinks that the rate of Newstart Allowance needs to be _____ .

2. What does Chris Richardson say about the wages and unemployment benefits in Australia?

He says, "We have one of the _____ minimum wages in the world and relative

to that, the _____ unemployment benefits."

3. What are two female ministers and the Prime Minister saying?

They are saying, "the best form of _____ is a _____ ."

PHASE 4

💬✍ Output Task (Writing / Speaking)

Unemployment Insurance (*i.e., Shitsugyo Hoken*「失業保険」, *officially known as Koyo Hoken*「雇用保険」), is available in Japan. Do some research about the insurance and write down two facts that you have learned about it. Then, share your findings with a partner and make a presentation in class.

Step I ▸ Do some research about unemployment insurance in Japan and write down two facts that you have learned about it on the next page.

> e.g.. • Who can join the insurance?
> • How much **Unemployment Benefits** do recipients get?
>   =Shitsugyo Teate「失業手当」, officially known as Kihon Teate「基本手当」
> • How long do they receive the benefits?
> • What should people do to apply for the benefits?

FINDINGS

- _____
  _____
- _____
  _____

---

e.g., • People who... are likely to be able to join the insurance.
- It looks like the amount of benefits is linked to....
- The duration of the benefits seems to depend on....
- People should... to apply for the benefits.

Step 2 Share your findings with your partner. Ask questions like *"What did you find out about unemployment insurance?"* and write down your partner's answers.

My partner found that _____

_____ .

He/She also found that _____

_____ .

Step 3 Practice the report that you made in Step 2. Then, present the report to the class.

Checklist for the Presentation

Use this checklist to evaluate one of your classmate's presentations.

		Good				Bad
1.	The speaker speaks in correct sentence forms.	5	4	3	2	1
2.	The speaker explains his/her partner's findings clearly.	5	4	3	2	1
3.	The speaker describes the findings in some detail.	5	4	3	2	1
4.	The speaker makes eye contact with the audience.	5	4	3	2	1

UNIT 7

Uncovering the Secrets of Water

Although water is one of the subjects which is included in most science education curricula all over the world, we do not know completely about this chemical compound. Where there is water, there could be life. Let's explore more about the secrets of water.

PHASE 1

1 | Getting into the Topic

Answer the following quizzes about water.

Try Water Quizzes!

Q1 Approximately, what percent of the human adult body is made up of water?

   a. 30%   **b.** 60%   **c.** 90%

Q2 Where did the first life on the Earth begin?

   a. River   **b.** Ocean   **c.** Iceberg

Q3 Why does an ice cube float in a glass of water?

   a. When water freezes, it shrinks and becomes less dense.
   b. When water freezes, it expands and becomes more dense.
   c. When water freezes, it expands and becomes less dense.

Q4 Which of the following cultural artifacts is NOT related to water?

   a. *The Great Wave* by Katsushika Hokusai
   b. *The Mona Lisa* by Leonardo da Vinci
   c. The Roman Bath in England

2 🎥◀ 1st Viewing

online / video

Watch the video and choose the best answers to the following questions.

1. What percentage of the Earth's surface is covered with water?
   a. 60%
   b. 70%
   c. 80%

2. Which of the following is NOT mentioned in the video?
   a. Without water, we don't have soil.
   b. Water helps keep our cells working.
   c. Water was found on Venus.

PHASE 2

1 📋 Vocabulary

Match the words with their definitions.

1. **insulate** [   ]   **a.** suitable for life to live in

2. **evolve** [   ]   **b.** to express an opinion about something without knowing all the details and facts

3. **spew up** [   ]

4. **speculate** [   ]   **c.** to develop gradually

5. **habitable** [   ]   **d.** to gradually increase in number or quantity over a period of time

6. **accumulate** [   ]   **e.** to cover something with a material that stops heat, sound, electricity, etc. from passing through

7. **impair** [   ]   **f.** to damage something or make something worse

   g. to send out in large quantities

2 📖 Reading

 DL 08   CD 08

Read the following passage.

Living with Water

There are 1.5 billion cubic kilometers of water on the Earth. It covers 70% of our planet's surface. We humans are in some sense, similar to the surface of the Earth, in that two-thirds

3   of our body weight is made up of water. We are surrounded by water in our daily lives.

It is said that water shaped the Earth and all life on it. How could that be possible? The answer lies in a fact everyone knows: ice floats in a glass of water because water expands when it freezes. As water repeatedly froze and melted over a long period of time, its powerful expansion shattered the rocks on the Earth to pieces, creating the perfect environment for life to grow. Since ice floats, it insulates the water underneath, giving life a place to survive and evolve. This is why all life started at the bottom of the ocean, where minerals and heat spewed up from inside the Earth and on to the sea floor.

Water exists not only on the Earth. Water has been found on the moon, on Mars, and there has been indication of water on the moons of Jupiter and Saturn. Actually, scientists have long speculated about the possibility of life on planets other than the Earth. In 2022, NASA announced that its rover has recently collected samples that include organic matter from Mars, which means the planet likely had a habitable environment 3.5 billion years ago.

Water not only creates a place to live, but also plays a crucial role inside our body. How does it work? Water in the body produces sweat to regulate body temperature. In addition, water circulates nutrients around our entire body and creates urine as a waste product. In other words, a lack of sweat and urine would cause the body's waste to accumulate. It would reduce the flow of blood, and impair the functions of the entire body, leading to death.

There are dozens of secrets related with water, but it is clear that it connects us with the universe. How to live wisely with this chemical compound may be one of the most important questions that we should ask about in our daily lives.

371 words

Notes

ℓ 13 **comet:** an object that moves around the sun, usually at a great distance from it, that is seen on rare occasions from the Earth as a bright line in the sky

ℓ 13 **Mars:** the fourth planet from the sun

ℓ 14 **Jupiter:** the fifth planet from the sun

ℓ 14 **Saturn:** the sixth planet from the sun

ℓ 18 **urine:** the pale yellow liquid released by the kidneys, containing waste products

3 📄 Organizer

Fill in each blank and complete the organizer based on the information from the reading.

Water: Facts and Roles It Plays

♂ **Key Facts**
- The percentage of water covering the surface of the Earth = [1] _____ %
- The proportion of water in our body = 2/3

How water shaped the life on the Earth

- Water expands when it freezes.
  - →Because it floats, it insulates the water underneath.
  - →It gave life a place to [2] _____ and evolve.

The relationship between water and life

Indication of water
- Water has been found on the [3] _____ , on Mars, etc.
  - →Possibility of life on a planet other than the Earth
- In 2022, NASA exploration showed that Mars likely had a [4] _____ environment 3.5 billion years ago.

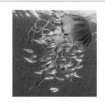

Water playing a crucial role in our [5] _____
- Water in the body produces sweat and urine:
  - →It helps regulate the body [6] _____ and prevent the body's waste from accumulating in the body.

What we should do

Ask about how to live [7] _____ with water: something that connects us with the universe

PHASE 3

2nd Viewing

Watch the video again and complete the answers to the following questions.

1. How did water help create the perfect environment for life to grow?

Water's powerful _____ shattered the rocks to pieces and gave life a place to

survive.

2. How does water work inside your body?

It nudges the _____ in proteins inside your cells to do their jobs, and shuffles

_____ and nutrients around you.

3. Along with water, what are the other three classical elements that exist in space?

_____ , _____ , and _____ .

PHASE 4

Output Task (Writing / Speaking)

We all know the importance of water. Humans can live for several weeks without food, but not without water. Do some research about water and write a short paragraph about what you have learned. Then, make a presentation in class.

Step 1 Do some research about water.

> e.g.
> · How much water do we need to drink daily?
> · Why is water so important for us human beings?
> · What do you think are the reasons for the lack of water in our world?

FINDINGS

· _____

_____

· _____

_____

Step 2 ▶ Write a short paragraph (about 30 words) about your findings. Give a title to the paragraph.

Title: _____

The most interesting thing I found out about water is _____

_____

_____

_____

e.g., Title: The importance of drinking water
The most interesting thing I found out about water is that it leaves my body when I sweat.
We need to drink water and circulate the water to stay healthy.

Step 3 ▶ Practice the report that you made in Step 2. Then, present the report to the class.

Checklist for the Presentation

Use this checklist to evaluate one of your classmate's presentations.

		Good				Bad
1.	The speaker speaks in correct sentence forms.	5	4	3	2	1
2.	The speaker explains his/her findings clearly.	5	4	3	2	1
3.	The speaker describes the findings in some detail.	5	4	3	2	1
4.	The speaker makes eye contact with the audience.	5	4	3	2	1

The Strategy to Prevent Obesity

There are people who suffer health problems from being overweight or obese. To solve these problems, the UK government and other countries are introducing a "sugar tax." Does it help people to adopt a more healthy diet? Let's find out the facts about the sugar tax.

PHASE 1

1 | Getting into the Topic

Read a brief summary of the "sugar tax" policy in the UK and choose the correct tax rate in the bracket for each of the two drinks.

The Soft Drinks Industry Levy: Summary

- ❷ Enacted in April 2018
- ❷ Requires manufacturers of sugary drinks to pay tax
- ❷ The rates are: 18 pence per liter if the drink has 5g of sugar or more per 100ml
  24 pence per liter if the drink has 8g of sugar or more per 100ml

---

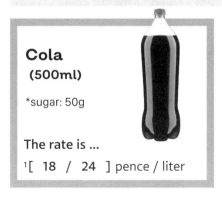

Cola
(500ml)

*sugar: 50g

The rate is ...
1[18 / 24] pence / liter

Energy Drink
(300ml)

*sugar: 36g

The rate is ...
2[18 / 24] pence / liter

2 🎥 1st Viewing

Watch the video and choose the best answers to the following questions.

1. In October 2011, which country introduced a tax on high-fat foods?

    a. Germany

    b. The US

    c. Denmark

2. Which is true about the speaker in the video?

    a. He agrees with a sugar tax.

    b. He disagrees with a sugar tax.

    c. He claims that sugar consumption is not bad for health.

PHASE 2

1 📋 Vocabulary

Match the words with their definitions.

1. diabetes [   ]   **a.** a medical condition in which the body cannot control the amount of sugar in the blood

2. implement [   ]   **b.** with each relating to something previously mentioned

3. inflation [   ]   **c.** a general, continuous rise in prices

4. absorb [   ]   **d.** an effort to bring information to people, especially to those who would not otherwise get it easily

5. alternative [   ]

6. respectively [   ]   **e.** to take something in; deal with the cost

7. outreach [   ]   **f.** to start something that has been officially decided

                         g. a thing that you can choose between two or more possibilities

2 📖 Reading

🎧 DL 09   💿 CD 09

Read the following passage.

Introducing "Sugar Tax" to Cut Obesity

    Obesity is causing a health crisis in many countries around the world. In the UK, for example, around 28% of adults are obese. Being overweight or obese makes people more
₃ likely to suffer health problems such as heart disease or diabetes. These diseases can affect a

person's quality of life or even cause early death. Obesity is mainly caused by a poor diet, so
5 many governments are considering a "sugar tax." They want to make unhealthy food more expensive so that people will eat more healthily.

Many people believe that a sugar tax is an effective way to reduce obesity. In the UK, more than 50% of people are in favor of a sugar tax. However, *the Guardian* data editor, Alberto Nardelli, points to the need to examine its potential negative impact more carefully.

10 First, flat indirect taxes such as a sugar tax are considered unfair. Poor people end up spending a larger percentage of their income on tax than rich people. People in the bottom 20% of earners spend around 37% of their income on "sin taxes" and VAT. However, the top 20% of people only spend 15%. It should also be noted that despite the high taxes, there is little evidence that people change their eating habits. Second, implementing extra flat indirect taxes
15 may cause price inflation and put jobs at risk. This was illustrated in Denmark in 2011. The Danish government introduced an extra tax on high-fat foods. However, they reversed their decision because food became so expensive that people crossed the border into Germany to buy food more cheaply. Third, a sugar tax may not be effective because sellers can just sell the unhealthy food cheaply and absorb the tax themselves in order to keep their customers. This
20 happened in California when a sugar tax was introduced.

Some examples show that public health and advertising campaigns that promote healthy alternatives to sweet food and drinks work better than a sugar tax. Howard County, in Maryland, US, managed to reduce sales of sodas and fruit juices by 20% and 15% respectively thanks to a combination of positive advertising of
25 healthy drinks and public outreach. This shows that there are ways of encouraging healthy eating without punishing people with taxes.

372 words

Notes

ℓ 10 **indirect tax:** a tax that can be passed on to another entity or individual; usually imposed on a manufacturer or supplier who then passes on the tax to the consumer. (e.g., tax on cigarettes and alcohol)

ℓ 10 **flat tax:** a tax system where everyone pays the same rate whether the person's income is high or low

ℓ 12 **sin tax:** a tax on socially harmful goods (e.g., alcohol, cigarettes, gambling, etc.)

ℓ 12 **VAT:** Value Added Tax; a tax that is added to the price of goods and services, and paid by the final customer

3 📄 Organizer

Fill in each blank and complete the organizer based on the information from the reading.

How Effective "Sugar Tax" Can Be

Background

Obesity is causing a ¹_____ crisis in many countries.
└ UK: Around ²_____ % of adults are obese.

▼

Introduction of a "sugar tax"
└ More than ³_____ % of people in the UK support it.

Guardian data editor's opinion

The need to examine the ⁴_____ impact of sugar tax

① Flat indirect taxes are considered unfair.
   └ Poor people spend more of their income on "sin taxes" and VAT than rich people.

② Sugar tax may cause price inflation and put jobs at ⁵_____.
   └ Denmark: An extra tax on high-fat foods was introduced in 2011.
   → Food became very expensive.
   → People crossed the border into Germany to buy food more cheaply.

③ Sellers sell unhealthy food cheaply and ⁶_____ the sugar tax themselves.
   └ They want to keep their customers.

A successful case: public health campaign

Howard County, Maryland, US

• Reduced sales of sodas and fruit juices by 20% and 15% respectively
   └ Thanks to advertising of healthy drinks and public ⁷_____
• Shows that sugar tax is not the only way to promote health

PHASE 3

2nd Viewing

online / video

Watch the video again and complete the answers to the following questions.

1. Whom do the flat indirect taxes hit the hardest?

They hit the _____ the hardest.

2. What happened when the sugar tax was introduced in Berkeley, California?

Only 22% of it was passed onto _____ .

3. Over the past decade, what has been falling in the US?

In the US, the _____ of _____ drinks has fallen by 25%
over the past decade.

PHASE 4

Output Task (Writing / Speaking)

When looking at the world rank of the obesity, Japan ranks low. However, when looking at the country itself, the cases of obesity are growing. Let's explore more about the problem, and make a presentation in class.

Step 1 What do you think are two reasons for increasing cases of obesity?

_____

_____

_____

e.g., The first reason that came to my mind is that many people skip breakfast.
Also, there is evidence that people spend less time doing exercise after the outbreak of COVID-19.

Step 2 How can we solve such problems?

_____

_____

_____

_____

e.g., People should try to go to sleep early and have breakfast before going to school/work.
If people try to do some exercise that they can do at home, it will help them keep fit.

Step 3 Practice the report that you made in Steps 1 and 2. Then, present the report to the class.

Checklist for the Presentation

Use this checklist to evaluate one of your classmate's presentations.

		Good				Bad
1.	The speaker speaks in correct sentence forms.	5	4	3	2	1
2.	The speaker gives clear reasons for obesity.	5	4	3	2	1
3.	The speaker provides a solution to the problem(s).	5	4	3	2	1
4.	The speaker makes eye contact with the audience.	5	4	3	2	1

Heated Debate on VAR

Recently, various opinions have arisen toward the use of VAR (Video Assistant Referee). Many people think that football games are enjoyable when you watch them live. Watch and listen to some journalists' opinions toward the use of VAR. What do you think?

PHASE 1

1 | Getting into the Topic

Read a quote by a former Argentine soccer player Diego Maradona. Then choose the best option to complete the summary of the famous "hand of god" goal.

"A little with the head of Maradona and a little with the hand of God."

—*Talking about the famous "hand of god" goal in the 1986 FIFA World Cup*

The hand of god: During the match between Argentina and ¹[France / England] in the 1986 FIFA World Cup, Maradona had jumped to ²[kick / head] the ball but ended up hitting it with his hand and went past the goalkeeper Peter Shilton to give Argentina a ³[lead / behind] of 1-0. It is said that the ⁴[referees / coaches] did not have a clear view of the play, but it is still a topic of debate.

2 |  1st Viewing

Watch the video and choose the best answers to the following questions.

1. Is this man for or against VAR?

    a. He is for the use of VAR.

    b. He is against the use of VAR.

    c. We cannot tell.

2. What does this man suggest?

    a. Using VAR during the match

    b. Using VAR after the match

    c. Both **a** and **b**

PHASE 2

1 | Vocabulary

Match the words with their definitions.

1. **penalty** [ ]   **a.** a punishment for doing something that is against a law or rule

2. **incident** [ ]   **b.** to make a situation less safe by causing changes and problems

3. **deceive** [ ]   **c.** to make someone believe that something false is the truth

4. **opponent** [ ]   **d.** affecting someone in a way that is annoying and uncomfortable

5. **intrusive** [ ]   **e.** a person who someone is competing against in a sports game, a competition, etc.

6. **resonate** [ ]

7. **destabilize** [ ]   **f.** to make you think of another similar value

  g. an event that is often unpleasant or unusual

2 | Reading

 DL 10   CD 10

Read the following passage.

Fans Give VAR the Yellow Card

    Video Assistant Referee (VAR) technology was officially used at the 2018 FIFA World Cup for the first time. Many people welcomed the decision to introduce VAR as they believed
³ it would cut down on the number of poor decisions made by referees and make the game

fairer for the players and the fans. In fact, early evidence from Italian football, where VAR had
5 been introduced on a trial basis before 2018, suggested that the use of VAR reduced refereeing
mistakes from 6% of decisions to under 1% of decisions.

VAR is not used for every decision. While there is always a referee watching the game
on the screens, VAR is only used to help the referee on the field in four "match-changing"
situations (and only the on-field referee can make the final decision). Those are goals, penalty
10 decisions, red-card incidents, and cases of mistaken identity of a player. According to a sports
journalist from *the Guardian*, what we don't necessarily notice about VAR is that now the
players know that their every move and behavior is being analyzed by VAR, and they are less
likely to try to deceive the on-field referee by diving or fouling opponents.

Now that VAR has been used over several seasons, what do the fans think? According
15 to a survey of 33,000 English Premier League fans, only 26% support the use of VAR. In fact,
95% of fans attending live matches replied that VAR has become too intrusive to the extent
that the experience of watching a game is less enjoyable: the introduction of VAR meant that
they could not celebrate goals as they were scored. One journalist's words resonate with the
fans' feelings: "Football is such a game of moments that come around infrequently, and they've
20 been so destabilized by the influence of VAR."

Despite its unpopularity, VAR is unlikely to be removed. Therefore, what could be done
to improve it? Some suggest letting the fans in the stadium see the video that is being reviewed
in real time and making them "involved" in
the game. One thing for sure is that further
25 discussion is needed so that the entertainment
value of the game is not lost forever.

364 words

Notes

ℓ 15 **English Premier League:** the top English professional football league

3 | 📄 Organizer

Fill in each blank and complete the organizer based on the information from the reading.

How People Reacted to VAR

⚽ **First Reaction**

- People welcomed the introduction of VAR in the 2018 FIFA World Cup.
- It would make the game fairer for both the [1]_____ and the fans.
  └ **Early evidence in Italian football:**
     VAR reduced refereeing mistakes from 6% of decisions to under 1%.

⚽ **How VAR works**

- It only helps the referee on the field in four "match-changing" situations.
  i.e., goals, [2]_____ decisions, red-card
     incidents, and cases of mistaken identity of a
     player

⚽ **Fans give VAR "the yellow card"**

English Premier League Fans
- 26% support the use of VAR.
- Almost all the supporters said that VAR made watching a game less enjoyable.
  └ They cannot [3]_____ goals as they were scored.

A journalist's words
- Football is a game where the "moments" are infrequent, and VAR [4]_____ these moments.

⚽ **The Future of VAR**

Suggestions
- Let the fans in the stadium see the video and make them "[5]_____" in the game
- Further [6]_____ is needed.

PHASE 3

◼◀ 2nd Viewing

online / video

Watch the video again and complete the answers to the following questions.

1. According to the Italian journalist, what does the evidence show so far?

   He says that the evidence suggests that VAR is _____ the number of wrong decisions in football.

2. What does the Italian journalist say is the biggest problem with VAR?

   He says that it is _____ with the _____ .

3. According to the German journalist, what should be done with the use of VAR?

   He suggests using VAR _____ the match to punish _____ .

PHASE 4

💬🖌 Output Task (Writing / Speaking)

There are various opinions toward the use of VAR. Imagine you are either (a) a football player, (b) a member of the audience at the stadium, or (c) the referee. Write down the pros and cons about the use of VAR. Then, share your opinion with a partner and make a presentation in class.

Step 1 ▶ Decide who you choose to be, and write down both a pro and con about the use of VAR.

_____

e.g., I am a football player.

Pro: _____

Con: _____

e.g., Pro: I think that using VAR will stop me from making fouls.
Con: I think that VAR makes the game boring.

Step 2 Share your thoughts with your partner. Then, write down the advantages and disadvantages mentioned by your partner.

My partner says that one advantage of VAR is _____

_____ .

One possible disadvantage he/she mentioned is _____

_____ .

I [agree/disagree] with his/her opinion.

Step 3 Practice the report that you made in Step 2. Then, present the report to the class.

Checklist for the Presentation

Use this checklist to evaluate one of your classmate's presentations.

		Good				Bad
1.	The speaker speaks in correct sentence forms.	5	4	3	2	1
2.	The speaker explains both advantages/disadvantages his/her partner mentioned.	5	4	3	2	1
3.	The speaker expresses agreement/ disagreement with his/her partner's views.	5	4	3	2	1
4.	The speaker makes eye contact with the audience.	5	4	3	2	1

UNIT 10

Lively Learning about Food Waste

The world is facing a big problem of food waste. In fact, tons of edible food are lost or wasted every day. We all have a part to play in saving food. How to reduce food waste might be one of the key issues that we should investigate.

PHASE 1

1 | Getting into the Topic

Read about a community garden space located in central London, and then complete the definitions of the underlined words by arranging the words in the brackets.

WELCOME TO THE SKIP GARDEN!

From 2009 to 2019, the Skip Garden was in the middle of the King's Cross development area. It was an urban oasis, as well as a unique space where apple trees, pumpkins, and beans grew out of **¹skips**. It helped people realize that they have a relationship with the land they are on, that they are not **²disconnected** from all of it.

Definitions:

1. skip: a large open [people / into which / put / container / unwanted stuff] or garden waste

_____

2. disconnected: [from / separate / else / something], and not fitting well together

_____

 1st Viewing

 online video

Watch the video and choose the best answers to the following questions.

1. What are the participants doing in the workshop?
   a. Cooking food
   b. Learning about food waste
   c. Both **a** and **b**

2. Which of the following foods was NOT mentioned in the video?
   a. Pudding
   b. French fries
   c. Stew

PHASE 2

1 Vocabulary

Match the words with their definitions.

1. **discard**   [   ] **a.** foods that are used together to make a particular dish
2. **nutritious**   [   ] **b.** containing many of the substances which help the body to stay healthy
3. **ingredients**   [   ] **c.** a particular way of thinking about something
4. **compost**   [   ] **d.** extremely interesting and attractive
5. **worm**   [   ] **e.** to throw something away that you no longer want or need
6. **fascinating**   [   ] **f.** a creature with a long, thin, soft body without arms, legs or bones
7. **perspective**   [   ] **g.** to make a mixture of decayed plants, food, etc., that can be added to soil to help plants grow

2 Reading

 DL 11   CD 11

Read the following passage.

Thinking Further into How to Reduce Food Waste

Food waste is an environmental problem that humans are facing. A considerable amount of edible food is discarded every day: from non-edible parts of vegetables to unsold or leftover
3 food that is still edible. As a result, a growing number of organizations or groups around the

world are trying to tackle this problem. One such group is Global Generation, an educational
charity based in London, which works together with local people and businesses to create a
healthy, integrated and environmentally responsible community. At the heart of their activities
is their "Garden" project. The community gardens they operate are located at several sites in
London (such as Camden, Islington, and Southwark), and one has offered space for growing
fruit and vegetables, as well as a café where nutritious and seasonal food is served. Various
workshops are regularly being held, too.

In one of their workshops, Global Generation invited a group of school children and
educated them on food waste. Rachel Solomon, the youth manager at Global Generation, says
that it may sometimes be surprising, but also understandable that the children living in the
cities do not really know about where their food comes from. They have never really had the
chance to realize the link between growing food and cooking.

After participating in this workshop, children learned about three things. Firstly, they
learned how to change the rubbish bin into a garden. Secondly, they learned how food waste
can be used in cooking. For example, they used many parts of food which is normally wasted
because they are slightly old or past its best. By using those ingredients for cooking and
turning them into puddings, stews or smoothies, children learned that they can still be made
into something really tasty, delicious, and nutritious. Lastly, they learned about composting.
As a compost, they used the food waste in a large skip, which includes a number of worms. By
mixing it with water and giving the water to plants, it can go back to nature, literally. When
children have learned how to compost, they realize the
fascinating points of nature.

As Rachel says, the workshop brings a new
perspective to the children.

359 words

Notes

ℓ 8 **Camden:** a district located in the inner northern part of London

ℓ 8 **Islington:** a district located in the inner northern part of London

ℓ 8 **Southwark:** a district located in the central part of London

3 | 📄 Organizer

Fill in each blank and complete the organizer based on the information from the reading.

Learning about Food Waste

The organizer of the workshop

Global Generation: an ¹_____ charity group which works together
with the local people
Organizing a "²_____" project
→They invited a group of school children and educated them on food waste.

Things children learned in the workshop

•**Gardening:** change the ³_____ bin into a
garden

•⁴_____: change the food waste into
something delicious and nutritious

•**Composting:** mix food waste, including ⁵_____, with water and give
the water to ⁶_____
→ It can go back to nature, literally.

What the organizer thinks

Rachel Solomon:
The workshop brings a new ⁷_____ to the children.

PHASE 3

2nd Viewing

online video

Watch the video again and complete the answers to the following questions.

1. How does one of the participants in the video describe a large skip in which plants are grown?

He says, "It's normally used for _____ rubbish in. You've _____

it into a garden."

2. What are the slightly old or out of date ingredients made into?

They are made into something really tasty, _____ , and _____ .

3. What does the boy making the stew say about food waste?

He says, "If they are wasting food, then they are _____ _____

away."

PHASE 4

Output Task (Writing / Speaking)

Given the effect of food waste on our environment, we should all think about how to reduce our food waste. In a group, think of three ways to reduce food waste. Then, present your ideas in front of the class.

Step I ▶ Brainstorm using a web drawn below.

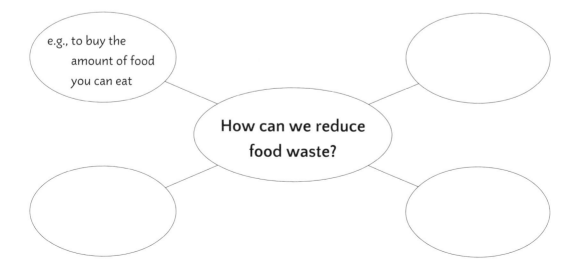

e.g., to buy the amount of food you can eat

How can we reduce food waste?

Step 2 Based on the web you have made on the previous page, write the script for the presentation. Fill in the blanks and complete the script below. Write a reason for each proposed way.

In our group, we thought of three ways to reduce food waste.

The first way is _____ .

By _____ .

The second way is _____ .

We think it is effective because _____ .

The last way is _____ .

It can help _____ .

We believe these actions will surely contribute to reducing food waste. Thank you for listening.

> e.g., The first way is to buy the amount of food that you can eat.
> By buying the portion you eat, you can save both food and money. ...

Step 3 Practice the report that you made in Step 2. Then, present the report to the class.

Checklist for the Presentation

Use this checklist to evaluate one of your classmate's presentations.

		Good				Bad
1.	The speaker speaks in correct sentence forms.	5	4	3	2	1
2.	The speaker describes three ways to reduce food waste.	5	4	3	2	1
3.	The speaker explains a reason for each proposed way.	5	4	3	2	1
4.	The speaker makes eye contact with the audience.	5	4	3	2	1

Inside an Underground Homeless Community

People try to find a comfortable place to live. In this case, the people in the video live underground. What made them decide to live in the underground world? Let's find out more about them by looking into their lives closely.

PHASE 1

1 | Getting into the Topic

The following is a ranking of the homeless population by US state. Referring to the map, fill in the names of the states that fit A–D from the choices below.

Source: United States Interagency Council on Homelessness

Homeless Population by State 2022

A _____	151,278
B _____	92,091
Florida	28,328
C _____	25,848
Washington	21,577

▶ Las Vegas is located in state of ᴰ _____ , which is ranked No. 19 (7,169 people).

California	Texas	New York	Nevada

2 | ◼️◀ 1st Viewing

online / video

Watch the video and choose the best answers to the following questions.

1. How many people are estimated to live underground?

   a. 100 people

   b. 200 people

   c. 300 people

2. How long has this man been down in the tunnel?

   a. Seven weeks

   b. Seven months

   c. Seven years

PHASE 2

1 | 📋 Vocabulary

Match the words with their definitions.

1. crisscross   [   ]   **a.** to live in a place or an environment

2. prone   [   ]   **b.** to cover something completely under water

3. downpour   [   ]   **c.** to move or exist in a pattern of cutting lines

4. submerge   [   ]   **d.** likely to get or liable to suffer from

5. infest   [   ]   **e.** to make something already bad even worse

6. inhabit   [   ]   **f.** heavy rainfall in a short time

7. exacerbate   [   ]   **g.** to cause damage or disease by being in large numbers

2 | 📖 Reading

🎧 DL 12   ◉ CD 12

Read the following passage.

Living Underground in Las Vegas

      Deep underground, a network of flood tunnels crisscrosses beneath the streets of Las Vegas. Although the city sits in the middle of a desert, it is prone to the occasional

3   downpour, causing flash floods. The tunnels redirect the water and prevent Las Vegas from

being submerged. In these tunnels live a community of people who have been forgotten by mainstream society. There are around 300 homeless people and most of them struggle with drug abuse and addiction. There is no electricity or clean water supply, the tunnels are infested with rats, and every time it rains, there is the danger of being swept away by floodwater.

Nobody is permitted to live in the tunnels, but the homeless people who inhabit them have managed to make it their home. They take furniture and equipment from waste containers to make a living space, and they use car batteries for light and to charge their mobile phones. A society has developed, with people cooperating to make their lives easier. They have even invented a series of codes in order to signal to the community when a police officer is coming, or if there is floodwater on its way.

One man who managed to escape from tunnel life is Paul Vautrinot. He lived in the flood tunnels for around three years when he was a drug addict. He spent that period of his life dealing and taking drugs and shoplifting in the stores directly above him. After getting arrested one day, he decided to enter drug court, and stay clean from then on. He then started volunteering at an organization which helps the people living in the tunnels. Now, he not only works to make the inhabitants comfortable, but offers to help them find a way back into society.

Las Vegas is not the only city in the US with a major homelessness problem. It is thought there are as many as one million homeless people in America. The causes of this are complicated, but a drug epidemic, a lack of low-cost housing, poor mental health care, and the recent pandemic have exacerbated a long-standing problem. The Las Vegas case casts a light on an ever-growing gap between the haves and have-nots in America.

370 words

Notes

ℓ 18 **drug court:** a drug rehabilitation program for people with criminal convictions

ℓ 24 **epidemic:** a widespread occurrence of a particular disease in a community

3 📄 Organizer

Fill in each blank and complete the organizer based on the information from the reading.

Living Underground in Las Vegas

Beneath the streets of Las Vegas

- A ¹_____ of flood tunnels crisscrosses the area beneath the city.
- Around 300 ²_____ people live there.
- No electricity or clean water supplies
- Rats run around in the place where they live.

Paul Vautrinot's case
- Became drug addicted and began living in the tunnels in Las Vegas
  → Survived by dealing drugs and ³_____
- Decided to face his drug addiction after getting
  ⁴_____
  → Now volunteering to help people who live in the tunnels

Homeless Problems in the US

Problem
- In America, there are as many as one million homeless people.
  └ The causes of this is due to a ⁵_____ epidemic, a lack of ⁶_____ housing, poor mental health care, and so on.

- Las Vegas case casts a light on an ⁷_____ gap between the haves and have-nots in America.

PHASE 3

◼◀ 2nd Viewing

Watch the video again and complete the answers to the following questions.

1. What kind of animals live in the tunnel?

There are bats, rats, and baseball-sized _____ .

2. According to Joel, why did a girl die last year?

Last February, she died in the _____ .

3. According to Joel, what do they need the batteries for?

To give them lights and plug in _____ _____ and sometimes
a hot plate.

PHASE 4

💬✔ Output Task (Writing / Speaking)

There are organizations to help struggling people survive in various ways. Do some
research about an organization that helps homeless people in Japan and write down
two ways how they help (support) them. Then, share your findings with a partner and
make a presentation in class.

Step I ▶ Do some research about one organization that helps homeless people in
Japan.

Name	_____ e.g., Homedoor
What kind of an organization is it?	It _____ e.g., It is a certified NPO (nonprofit organization).
When was it established?	It _____ e.g., It was established in 2010.
How do they help/ support homeless people? (Give two ways)	•They _____ •They _____ e.g., They carry out "Night Patrol" once a month. They offer a room for people who do not have a place to stay for free.

Step 2 Write a report (about 40 words) about the organization. Use the information you answered in Step 1.

I am going to report on _____

_____

_____

_____

> e.g., I am going to report on an organization named Homedoor. It is a certified NPO established in 2010. They carry out "Night Patrol" once a month and offer a room for people who do not have a place to stay for free.

Step 3 Practice the report that you made in Step 2. Then, present the report to the class.

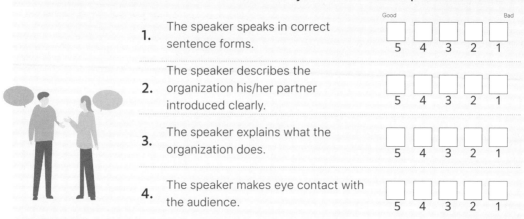

Checklist for the Presentation

Use this checklist to evaluate one of your classmate's presentations.

		Good				Bad
1.	The speaker speaks in correct sentence forms.	5	4	3	2	1
2.	The speaker describes the organization his/her partner introduced clearly.	5	4	3	2	1
3.	The speaker explains what the organization does.	5	4	3	2	1
4.	The speaker makes eye contact with the audience.	5	4	3	2	1

Women's Rights and AI Development

Artificial intelligence (AI) makes our lives more efficient. However, it could also be a threat to humankind, particularly women. In the video, Jeanette Winterson, a British writer, reads an extract from her book, in which she describes women's history and raises an important question: Where will women be in the future?

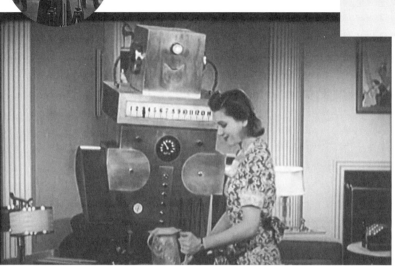

PHASE 1

1 | Getting into the Topic

Figure **A** shows the number of male/female MPs (Members of Parliament) in the UK, and Figure **B** shows the proportion of male/female students in four science and technology fields at the UK universities. Answer the following questions.

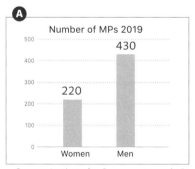

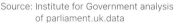

Source: Institute for Government analysis of parliament.uk.data

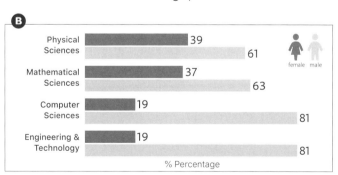

Source: 2017 STEM Women Limited

1. Look at Figure **A**. What percentage of the MPs are women as of 2019?   About _____%

2. Look at Figure **B**. Name two fields where the percentage of male students are more than twice that of female students.

_____   _____

2 ◻◀ 1st Viewing

online video

Watch the video and choose the best answers to the following questions.

1. Which AI products are mainly introduced in the video?
   a. Self-driving cars
   b. Security cameras
   c. Robots

2. What events are being held on the street?
   a. Women's music festivals
   b. Women's marches
   c. Both **a** and **b**

PHASE 2

1 📋 Vocabulary

Match the words with their definitions.

1. **entrepreneur** [   ]   **a.** having more power or influence than other things

2. **pose** [   ]   **b.** to totally change the way of something

3. **dominance** [   ]   **c.** the intentional act of not including someone/something

4. **revolutionize** [   ]   **d.** doing the same thing again and again

5. **repetitive** [   ]   **e.** treated as less important or of lower rank

6. **exclusion** [   ]   **f.** a person who builds a fortune by starting or running businesses

7. **inferior** [   ]   **g.** to create a problem or difficulty

2 📖 Reading

🎧 DL 13   ⊙ CD 13

Read the following passage.

Where Will Women Be in the Future?

In 1903, the Women's Social and Political Union (WSPU), known as the Suffragettes, was founded in Manchester, the UK. They had been fighting to win the rights to vote. In 1928, women aged 21 and over achieved the same voting rights as men. Now, women have become players in various fields. They are lawyers, doctors, scientists, journalists, artists, economists, entrepreneurs, astronauts, and politicians. Two hundred eight women MPs were elected at the 2017 General Election in the UK. Based on these facts, it looked like the women's rights movement had been completed, at least in the Western world. However, Jeanette Winterson, a British writer, expressed her concern in her book, *Courage Calls to Courage Everywhere*, that there would be the threat to women posed by the future dominance of AI.

Ms. Winterson mentioned that AI could be the best thing to happen to humans. For example, AI robot "Sophia," created by Hanson Robotics, can promote products, provide customer services, and so on. According to the writer, robots are tools and could revolutionize the world of work. They do repetitive jobs instead of humans. On the other hand, the writer also stated that AI could be the worst thing to happen to women. It looks like computer science remains a male-dominated field. The writer indicated that women accounted for only about 18% of computer science graduates. She warned that the future dominance of AI could be a threat to women and that we should not allow the future to become a new exclusion zone for women.

Women in the 21st century are still active in the women's rights movement. On January 21, 2017, the day after the former US president Donald Trump took office, hundreds of thousands of women gathered in Washington, D.C. to defend women's rights. The protests also took place throughout the US and other countries for gender equality, civil rights, and so on. Ms. Winterson claimed that women were not inferior and that they belonged in the world. The writer called for women to "Speak it. Write it. Read it. Make it visible. Let it be heard," and "Let courage call to courage everywhere."

356 words

Notes

ℓ 1   **suffragette:** a woman who was involved in the campaign for women's rights to vote

ℓ 5   **MP:** the abbreviation for 'Member of Parliament' (a person elected to represent the people of a particular area in the country)

ℓ 12   **Hanson Robotics:** a Hong Kong-based humanoid robotics company

3 📄 Organizer

Fill in each blank and complete the organizer based on the information from the reading.

Women's Rights Movement

Past	•The foundation of ¹ _____ _____ in the UK, 1903 •Voting rights for women aged ² ____ and over in 1928

▼

Present & Future	•Women's participation in the workplace and politics └ e.g., 208 women ³ _____ ⚠ **The threat to women posed by the future dominance of ⁴ ____** ⁴ ____ —The BEST thing to happen to humankind? e.g., AI Robot "⁵ _____" ⁴ ____ —The ⁶ _____ thing to happen to women? e.g., computer science └ a ⁷ _____ -dominated field •Women's march in the US and other countries •*"Let courage call to courage everywhere"* (by Jeanette Winterson)

PHASE 3

◼◀ 2nd Viewing

Watch the video again and complete the answers to the following questions.

1. How many women MPs were there a hundred years ago?

There were _____ women MPs.

2. What does the speaker say about the low rate (i.e., 18%) of female computer science graduates?

She says, "this is nothing to do with women's hard-wired aptitude for _____ or

_____."

3. What does the speaker suggest about the word "history?"

She suggests that "history" should include _____ - _____ .

PHASE 4

💬✔ Output Task (Writing / Speaking)

AI makes our lives easier, but it could also be a danger to us. Write down your thoughts about advantages OR disadvantages of AI applications. Then, share your thoughts with a partner and make a presentation in class.

Step 1 ▶ Write a short paragraph (about 30 words) describing advantages OR disadvantages of AI applications with examples.

Advantages	AI applications _____ _____ . For example, _____ _____ _____ . e.g., AI applications can be helpful for our daily lives. For example, Amazon Alexa, a voice-controlled digital or virtual assistant program that uses AI technology, can help us in the kitchen, finding recipes and giving us voice-guided directions.
Disadvantages	AI applications _____ _____ . For example, _____ _____ _____ . e.g., AI applications would lead to unemployment. For example, Fukoku Mutual Life Insurance, a Japanese insurance company, replaced employees with an AI system that can calculate insurance payouts.

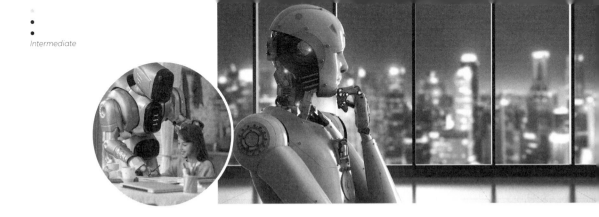

Step 2 ▸ Share your thoughts with your partner. Write down the advantages OR disadvantages mentioned by your partner.

My partner says that one [advantage / disadvantage] of AI applications is _____

_____ . He/She explains that _____

_____

_____ .

I [agree / disagree] with his/her opinion.

Step 3 ▸ Practice the report that you made in Step 2. Then, present the report to the class.

Checklist for the Presentation

Use this checklist to evaluate one of your classmate's presentations.

		Good				Bad
1.	The speaker speaks in correct sentence forms.	5	4	3	2	1
2.	The speaker explains an advantage or disadvantage of AI applications clearly.	5	4	3	2	1
3.	The speaker explains his/her partner's view with an example.	5	4	3	2	1
4.	The speaker makes eye contact with the audience.	5	4	3	2	1

Fighting Hair Discrimination and Racism

For a long time, some people have been treated in an unfair way based on their hairstyles. This is often called "hair discrimination." There seems to be racism (i.e., the unfair treatment of people based on their race) behind hair discrimination.

PHASE 1

1 | Getting into the Topic

The following are typical hairstyles for black people. Read each description and choose the name that best describes each photo from below.

(ᴬ   )

a hairstyle in which the hair is worn in long, ropelike locks

(ᴮ   )

a hairstyle of tight curls in a full evenly rounded shape

(ᶜ   )

a hairstyle in which the hair is braided usually flat to the scalp

mohawk	dreadlocks	cornrows	perm	afro

2 | ◼◀ 1st Viewing

(online / video)

Watch the video and choose the best answers to the following questions.

1. Who most likely is this woman?
   a. A school teacher
   b. An anti-discrimination activist
   c. A popular hairstylist

2. At the end of the video, what news is shared by this anchorwoman?
   a. A new law
   b. A new government
   c. A new hairstyle

PHASE 2

1 | 📋 Vocabulary

Match the words with their definitions.

1. **subtle**   [   ]   **a.** to state that something is not allowed
2. **textured**   [   ]   **b.** very unpleasant or so bad that it cannot be accepted
3. **ban**   [   ]   **c.** to make a strong request that something be done
4. **distract**   [   ]   **d.** not obvious, not attracting attention to itself
5. **traumatize** [   ]   **e.** to shock someone very much and make them worried or unhappy
                              for a long time
6. **disgusting** [   ]
                            f. having a surface that is rough, not smooth
7. **urge**   [   ]
                            g. to attract someone's attention to a different direction

2 | 📖 Reading

🎧 DL 14   ⦿ CD 14

Read the following passage.

Hair Discrimination: A Subtle Form of Racism

Although around 87% of the UK population is white European, there is a growing minority of Britons with black African, Caribbean, or mixed heritage. According to the
3 Equality Act 2010, it is illegal to discriminate against people because of their race. However

recently, more people are becoming aware of "hair discrimination," which is a more subtle
5 form of racial discrimination.

People of black African origin tend to have thick, tightly curled and textured hair.
Throughout history, they have taken this into account by braiding their hair or wearing it
in dreadlocks. The famous afro hairstyle then emerged in the 1960s as a symbol of pride
for people of African origin. However, in white-majority cultures, these hairstyles are often
10 considered "extreme," and are often banned in schools and workplaces. Ruby Williams, a
student, told *the Guardian* that she was sent home for simply wearing her curly hair in its
natural state. She was told that her hair was too big and would distract other students.

Zina Alfa, British activist, says that she was traumatized by her experience as a 12-year-
old girl when her teacher told her that her braided hair was ugly and disgusting. Over time,
15 however, she learned to love her hair through understanding the history behind it: curly hair
evolved to protect people from the sun in hot climates so that it does not absorb sweat. Now,
Zina is actively working to end hair discrimination. Her mission is to create a society where
people can feel confident with the hair they were born with.

In 2021, a group of MPs and campaigners including Zina signed a letter to urge the
20 UK government to recognize afro-textured hair as a protected characteristic. There is also
a growing movement among hairstylists for protecting afro hair. For a long time, people
with afro hair have had to go to special salons to get their hair cut, but in order to change
the situation, a natural hairstylist based in London started an academy for teaching stylists
how to cut and style textured afro hair. She hopes that all hairdressers, whether they have
25 European, African, or any other origin, will be
able to cut and style afro hair in the near future.

367 words

Notes

ℓ 2   **Briton:** a person from Britain, the island including England, Scotland, and Wales

ℓ 2   **Caribbean:** relating to the Caribbean Sea and its islands, or to people in the region

ℓ 2   **mixed heritage:** having parents from different racial groups

ℓ 2   **the Equality Act 2010:** an act that legally protects you against discrimination in the workplace and in wider society

3 | 📄 Organizer

Fill in each blank and complete the organizer based on the information from the reading.

Hair Discrimination in the UK

> a majority of white Europeans
> a minority of non-white Britons

Hairstyles of people having black African origin

- These people tend to have thick, tightly ¹_____ and textured hair.
- → They braid their hair or wear it in dreadlocks.
- → Afro hairstyles emerged in the ²_____ as a symbol of pride for them.

Hair discrimination

- These hairstyles are often banned in ³_____ and workplaces.

e.g., Ruby Williams was sent home from school for wearing her
curly hair in its natural state.

e.g., Zina Alfa was told by her teacher that her braided hair was
ugly and ⁴_____.

- Zina learned to love her hair through understanding the ⁵_____ behind it.

e.g., Curly hair evolved to protect people from the sun in hot
climates so that it does not absorb sweat.

Movements to end hair discrimination

- MPs and campaigners including Zina urged the ⁶_____ to recognize afro hair as a protected characteristic.
- ⁷_____ are trying to protect afro hair.

e.g., an academy for teaching stylists how to cut and style afro
hair

PHASE 3

🔲◀ 2nd Viewing

Watch the video again and complete the answers to the following questions.

1. What does Zina Alfa indicate about hair discrimination?

It is not based on _____ bias, but it is actually rather a conduit (i.e., a means of

passing information) for _____ discrimination.

2. According to Zina, what happened to slaves who were brought into the West and forced to work?

Their hair was _____ off as a form of cultural assimilation.

3. According to Zina, which places have created specific laws to protect people against hair

discrimination?

Places like New York and _____ have created these laws.

PHASE 4

💬✓ Output Task (Writing / Speaking)

Like Zina Alfa, people have been fighting racism. Do some research about
organizations that fight racism. Create a report and make a presentation about one
organization of your interest.

Step 1 ▶ Choose one organization and summarize the information below.

1	Name	e.g., The National Association for the Advancement of Colored People (NAACP)
2	Establishment/ Foundation (i.e., country and year)	e.g., the U.S., 1909
3	Major Accomplishments	e.g., worked for the end of racial segregation (i.e., the policy of separating one group from another) in public schools

Intermediate

Step 2 ▶ Write a report (about 40 words) about the organization. Use the information you answered in Step 1.

I am going to report on _____

_____

_____

_____

> e.g., I am going to report on the National Association for the Advancement of Colored People (NAACP). It was founded in the US in 1909. It worked for the end of racial segregation in public schools, and black children could eventually go to the same schools as white children.

Step 3 ▶ Practice the report that you made in Step 2. Then, present the report to the class.

Checklist for the Presentation

Use this checklist to evaluate one of your classmate's presentations.

		Good				Bad
1.	The speaker speaks in correct sentence forms.	5	4	3	2	1
2.	The speaker explains the basic information (name, establishment/ foundation, etc.) of the organization clearly.	5	4	3	2	1
3.	The speaker explains the organization's accomplishment(s).	5	4	3	2	1
4.	The speaker makes eye contact with the audience.	5	4	3	2	1

Intermediate

UNIT 14
Ways to Get Out of Busyness Trap

Recently, telling someone "how busy you are" seems to be natural, but are we always so busy, literally? We all know that we should rest and take care of ourselves. Why is it becoming difficult in the modern world? Let's look at what busyness really is and the ways to get out of the "busyness trap."

PHASE 1

1 | Getting into the Topic

The graph below the photos shows the results of a survey on how Americans manage stress. First, fill in the blanks with the appropriate verbs to describe the photos, and then guess which photos from A–D fit blanks 1–4 in the graph.

A P _____

B E _____

C L _____ to music

D Y _____

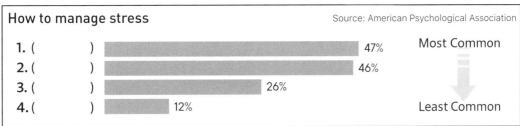

How to manage stress Source: American Psychological Association

1. ( ) ████████████ 47% Most Common
2. ( ) ████████████ 46%
3. ( ) ███████ 26%
4. ( ) ████ 12% Least Common

 **1st Viewing**

Watch the video and choose the best answers to the following questions.

1. What does the speaker say life is like?

    a. Going on a trip

    b. Packing for a trip

    c. Selecting a suitcase

2. Who gets the easier life?

    a. People who are efficient with their work

    b. People who are lazy

    c. Both **a** and **b**

PHASE 2

1 Vocabulary

Match the words with their definitions.

1. brag   [   ]   **a.** to make someone feel they are expected to do something

2. juggle   [   ]   **b.** to try to deal with two or more things at the same time

3. infinite   [   ]   **c.** seeming difficult to understand because it involves two contrary facts or qualities

4. oblige   [   ]

5. mindset   [   ]   **d.** without limits; endless in space, extent, or size

6. paradoxical   [   ]   **e.** the situation in which there is something more than you need

7. abundance   [   ]   **f.** to talk too proudly about what you have done or what you own

                              g. a way that someone thinks and feels

2 Reading  DL 15   CD 15

Read the following passage.

Busyness as Usual

    In the modern world, we often tell each other how busy we are. Many people are annoyed by this because it sounds like "busy-bragging." That is, busyness can almost be
3 considered a way of showing off how important you are, because it implies that you are

juggling a high-status job, a family, household, and hobbies.

5   Even people who do not "busy-brag" feel overwhelmed with the number of tasks they have to complete. In the past, when most people worked on farms or in other physical jobs, the amount we could do in a day was limited by our physical resources. In contrast, these days, when so many people work with infinite information and constant connectivity, there is no limit to the amount we can do. As a result, we find ourselves getting stuck in a "busyness

10 trap" that is hard to get out of.

     The first step to get out of this is to realize what busyness really is. Although modern people always feel busy, evidence suggests that we actually have far more leisure time than the generations before us. The feeling of busyness, therefore, is just that—a feeling. We feel obliged to say we are busy to avoid being thought of as lazy and talking about our busyness

15 makes us feel even worse.

     Now that you realize what busyness is, you may wonder how you can get over the feeling of it. Actually, the simplest but most effective advice is just "change your mindset." If we naturally accept that it is impossible to do everything within a limited amount of time, we will figure out the things that absolutely must be done and let go of the rest. Paradoxical

20 as it may seem, there is research suggesting that people can gain a sense of "time abundance" when they give away some of their time, for example, to volunteering. You will be satisfied by the fact that you can efficiently achieve something useful, and this will make you more confident in handling multiple tasks when you get back to work. So, the next time you feel overwhelmed with tasks in front of you, why don't you shift your focus from "how busy

25 you are" onto "what you can achieve" within what seems an impossibly short space of time?

379 words

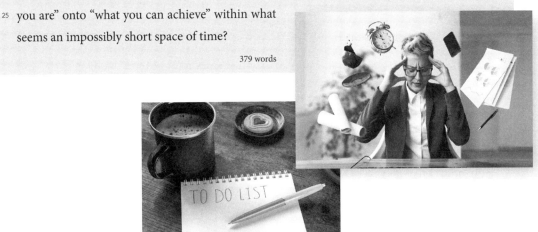

Note

ℓ 3   **show off:** to behave in a way intended to attract attention or to impress others by talking about your abilities, possessions, etc.

3 📄 Organizer

Fill in each blank and complete the organizer based on the information from the reading.

How to Get Out of "Busyness Trap"

In the Past	• People worked on farms or in other physical jobs. └ Working time was ¹_____ by one's physical resources.	

⬇

In the Modern World	• "Busy bragging" → ²_____ off how important you are → Implying that you are juggling a high-status job, a family, household, and hobbies • People work with infinite information and constant ³_____. → No limit to the amount we can do → Getting ⁴_____ in a "busyness trap"	

⬇

• *Solution* •

 ❶ Realize what busyness really is
• We have more ⁵_____ time than the past generations.
• Feeling of busyness is just a feeling.

 ❷ Change your ⁶_____
• Accept that it is impossible to do everything
• People will gain a sense of "time ⁷_____"
  by using time for something useful such as volunteering.

⬇

You will feel satisfied and confident.

PHASE 3

◼◀ 2nd Viewing

Watch the video again and complete the answers to the following questions.

1. What does it mean that "life is a bit like packing a suitcase for a trip?"

It means that we have a fixed amount of _____ and a fixed amount of

_____ to try to fit in our life.

2. What is the idea of "compartmentalized time?"

It is the idea of putting _____ around parts of time and trying to do just one

thing in each period.

3. What is the big takeaway that the speaker states?

He says that to solve the busyness problem, it is important to _____ that you

cannot get everything done.

PHASE 4

💬✎ Output Task (Writing / Speaking)

Some people may feel they are stuck in the busyness trap. When do you feel overwhelmed? How do you cope with such stress? Answer the questions below. Then, share your answers with a partner and make a presentation in class.

Step I ▶ Write down when you feel overwhelmed and how you cope with such stress.

When do you feel overwhelmed?	I feel overwhelmed (when) _____ _____ _____ e.g., I feel overwhelmed when constantly looking at my phone and checking notifications.
How do you cope with such stress?	I try to relax myself (by) _____ _____ _____ e.g., I try to relax myself by hiding my phone and not checking the screen.

Step 2 Share your answers with your partner. Ask the two questions from the previous page and write down your partner's answers.

_____ feels overwhelmed when _____
(your partner's name)

_____ .

He/She tries to relax him/herself by _____

_____ .

Step 3 Practice the report that you made in Step 2. Then, present the report to the class.

Checklist for the Presentation

Use this checklist to evaluate one of your classmate's presentations.

		Good				Bad
1.	The speaker speaks in correct sentence forms.	☐ 5	☐ 4	☐ 3	☐ 2	☐ 1
2.	The speaker explains clearly when his/her partner feels busy.	☐ 5	☐ 4	☐ 3	☐ 2	☐ 1
3.	The speaker explains the way his/her partner tries to relax.	☐ 5	☐ 4	☐ 3	☐ 2	☐ 1
4.	The speaker makes eye contact with the audience.	☐ 5	☐ 4	☐ 3	☐ 2	☐ 1

Video Credit

All the videos in *INTEGRITY* are originally taken from *the Guardian*.

Unit 1 Taste test: meat-free v plant-based 'meat' burgers (October 20, 2019)
www.theguardian.com/global/video/2019/oct/21/taste-test-meat-free-and-plant-based-meat-burgers-video

Unit 2 The Green Recovery: how to put more electric vehicles on Australia's roads (July 29, 2020)
www.theguardian.com/australia-news/video/2020/jul/29/the-green-recovery-how-to-put-more-electric-cars-on-the-road-video

Unit 3 Keep your chia seed smoothies off my Instagram feed (October 14, 2015)
www.theguardian.com/commentisfree/video/2015/oct/14/keep-your-chia-seed-smoothies-off-my-instagram-feed-video

Unit 4 How can I relax in job interviews? (April 10, 2015)
www.theguardian.com/lifeandstyle/video/2015/apr/10/how-relax-job-interviews-agony-aunt-video

Unit 5 'When we walk in, people's faces light up': training dogs to be pet therapists (December 30, 2015)
www.theguardian.com/lifeandstyle/video/2015/dec/30/animal-therapy-mayo-clinic-new-york-therapy-animals-video

Unit 6 'It's literally like counting your coins': the growing momentum to raise Newstart (August 3, 2019)
www.theguardian.com/global/video/2019/aug/03/its-literally-like-counting-your-coins-the-growing-momentum-to-raise-newstart-video-explainer

Unit 7 Water: the strangest chemical in the universe (May 28, 2015)
www.theguardian.com/science/video/2015/may/28/water-strangest-chemical-universe-explainer-video

Unit 8 Would a sugar tax even work? The facts you need to know (November 11, 2015)
www.theguardian.com/commentisfree/video/2015/nov/11/sugar-tax-facts-need-to-know-video

Unit 9 Will video assistant refereeing improve football? (June 16, 2018)
www.theguardian.com/football/video/2018/jun/16/will-video-assistant-refereeing-improve-football-video

Unit 10 Food waste: children's gardening and cookery workshop (March 2, 2014)
www.theguardian.com/lifeandstyle/video/2014/mar/02/live-better-challenge-food-waste-video

Unit 11 'I came down here to be forgotten': life in the tunnels beneath Las Vegas (November 22, 2017)
www.theguardian.com/us-news/video/2017/nov/22/las-vegas-homeless-tunnels-forgotten-outside-in-america

Unit 12 Is AI the 'worst thing to ever happen to women?' (March 8, 2019)
www.theguardian.com/world/video/2019/mar/08/is-ai-the-worst-thing-to-ever-happen-to-women-video

Unit 13 How can we help end hair discrimination? (March 16, 2021)
www.theguardian.com/world/video/2021/mar/16/hair-discrimination-video-explainer

Unit 14 I'm too busy! How can we get out of this busyness trap? (December 31, 2014)
www.theguardian.com/commentisfree/video/2014/dec/31/too-busy-busyness-trap

Photo Credit

このテキストのメインページ
www.kinsei-do.co.jp/plusmedia/41

次のページの QR コードを読み取る
直接ページにジャンプできます

オンライン映像配信サービス「plus⁺Media」について

本テキストの映像は plus⁺Media ページ（www.kinsei-do.co.jp/plusmedia）から、ストリーミング再生でご利用いただけます。手順は以下に従ってください。

ログイン

● ご利用には、ログインが必要です。
サイトのログインページ（www.kinsei-do.co.jp/plusmedia/login）へ行き、plus⁺Media パスワード（次のページのシールをはがしたあとに印字されている数字とアルファベット）を入力します。

● パスワードは各テキストにつき1つです。
有効期限は、<u>はじめてログインした時点から1年間</u>になります。

ログインページ

[利用方法]

次のページにある QR コード、もしくは plus⁺Media トップページ（www.kinsei-do.co.jp/plusmedia）から該当するテキストを選んで、そのテキストのメインページにジャンプしてください。

メニューページ　　　再生画面

plus+Media トップ　　　メインページ

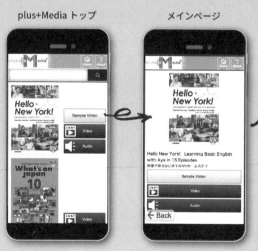

「Video」「Audio」をタッチすると、それぞれのメニューページにジャンプしますので、そこから該当する項目を選べば、ストリーミングが開始されます。

[推奨環境]

iOS (iPhone, iPad)	OS: iOS 12 以降 ブラウザ：標準ブラウザ	Android	OS: Android 6 以降 ブラウザ：標準ブラウザ、Chrome
PC	OS: Windows 7/8/8.1/10, MacOS X　ブラウザ：Internet Explorer 10/11, Microsoft Edge, Firefox 48以降, Chrome 53以降, Safari		

※最新の推奨環境についてはウェブサイトをご確認ください。
※上記の推奨環境を満たしている場合でも、機種によってはご利用いただけない場合もあります。また、推奨環境は技術動向等により変更される場合があります。予めご了承ください。

本書にはCD（別売）があります

INTEGRITY　Intermediate

Vitalize Your English Studies with Authentic Videos

海外メディア映像から深める　４技能・教養英語【中級編】

2023年 1 月20日　初版第 1 刷発行
2023年 2 月20日　初版第 2 刷発行

編著者　　　竹　内　　　理

薮　越　知　子

新　原　由　希　恵

Brent Cotsworth

発行者　　　福　岡　正　人

発行所　　株式会社　金　星　堂

（〒101-0051）　東京都千代田区神田神保町 3-21
Tel　（03）3263-3828（営業部）
（03）3263-3997（編集部）
Fax　（03）3263-0716
https://www.kinsei-do.co.jp

編集担当　蔦原美智・長島吉成　　　　　　　　Printed in Japan
印刷所・製本所／萩原印刷株式会社

ISBN978-4-7647-4175-1　C1082